Volume XIV, Number 5

Significant Issues Series

The Church in Contemporary Mexico

by George W. Grayson

foreword by M. Delal Baer

The Center for Strategic
and International Studies
Washington, D.C.

Library of Congress Cataloging-in-Publication Data

Grayson, George W., 1938–
    The Church in contemporary Mexico / by George W. Grayson.
        p. cm. — (Significant issues series, ISSN 0736-7136; v. 14, no. 5)
    Includes bibliographical references.
    ISBN 0-89206-182-0
    1. Catholic Church—Mexico—History—1965- 2. Mexico—Church
history—20th century. 3. Church and state—Mexico. I. Title. II. Series
    BX1428.2.G74 1992
    282'.72—dc20   91-36398
                                          CIP

Contents

About the Author

George W. Grayson is the Class of 1938 Professor of Government at the College of William and Mary in Williamsburg, Virginia. His writings include *The Politics of Mexican Oil* (1980), *The United States and Mexico: Patterns of Influence* (1984), *Oil and Mexican Foreign Policy* (1988), *Prospects for Mexico* (1988), *The Mexican Labor Machine:Power, Politics, and Patronage* (1989), and *Prospects for Democracy in Mexico* (1990).

His articles have appeared in the *Christian Science Monitor, Commonweal, Foreign Policy,* the *Journal of Commerce,* the *Journal of Inter-American Studies and World Affairs,* the *Los Angeles Times,* the *New Republic, Newsday, Orbis,* the *San Diego Union,* the *Wall Street Journal,* and the *Washington Post.*

Grayson, who has made 25 research trips to Mexico since 1976, lectures regularly at the National War College, the Army War College, and the Foreign Service Institute of the U.S. Department of State.

Grayson holds degrees from the University of North Carolina (B.A.), the Paul H. Nitze School of Advanced International Studies of the Johns Hopkins University (M.A. and Ph.D.), and the College of William and Mary (J.D.). He is a member of Phi Beta Kappa.

He has served as a member of the state legislature of Virginia for 18 years.

Foreword

If a Mexican Rip Van Winkle were to awaken in 1992 after slumbering 20 years, he would rub his eyes in disbelief. He would see that his country's youthful president, Carlos Salinas de Gortari, had rolled out the red carpet for foreign investors who had been viewed as a threat to national sovereignty in the early 1970s when the mercurial Luis Echeverria Alvarez occupied the presidential palace. Salinas and his predecessor, Miguel de la Madrid, had also tumbled the high walls of protectionism to open the way for a flood of imports, even as Mexican entrepreneurs—attuned as never before to competition— honed their export capability. He would hear proposals to link Mexico's economy with the United States and Canada in a North American Free Trade Agreement—a previously unthinkable concept because it evoked images of Yankee imperialism. He would find on the books a new law permitting peasants to rent, combine, and even sell their *ejidos* or communal holdings that had been regarded as sacrosanct by politicians from across the political spectrum. He would discover that the once redoubtable chieftain of the venal Oil Workers Union languished in prison as part of the chief executive's campaign to quash corruption and spur efficiency in the petroleum sector. Also behind bars were businessmen who had evaded tax payments—a crime previously considered about as serious as jaywalking is in the United States.

Equally astonishing to the newly aroused observer would be the changes in the political realm. Youthful, bright, foreign-educated technocrats dominated the cabinet that had formerly been the bailiwick of jowly, veteran politicos. Opposition parties boasted 40 percent of the seats in the Chamber of Deputies where the ruling Institutional Revolutionary Party (PRI) had previously held 9 out of 10 places. And members of the center-right National Action Party possessed two governorships and were poised to capture a third in a country in which the PRI had monopolized statehouses for 60 years after the party's creation in 1929.

As amazing as anything to the long dormant Mexican would be the new status of the Roman Catholic church. When he lay his head on the pillow, the church had been an inviting target continually attacked by intellectuals, union activists, leftist politicians, and PRI spokesmen. Such treatment sprang from the church's identification with the administration of Porfirio Díaz (1876–1911) and its opposition to the regime that emerged in the wake of the dictator's overthrow. The anti-clerical revolutionary constitution of 1917 eliminated the church's legal standing, severely curtailed its role in education, restricted the activities of priests who could no longer wear religious garb in public, and forbade outdoor worship services.

By 1992 the status of the church had changed. At President Salinas's initiative, the constitution had been amended to normalize church-state relations. This reform recognized the church's juridical status, authorized a broader role for it in education, allowed the clergy to vote and criticize the government, legalized the presence of foreign priests in the country, and permitted religious bodies to disseminate their views through the mass media. In addition, it appeared only a matter of time before diplomatic relations between Mexico and the Vatican, severed amid the Liberal reforms of the 1850s, would be restored. After all, Pope John Paul II had traveled to Mexico in May 1990, Salinas had visited the Vatican 14 months later, and the two leaders had exchanged "personal envoys." Meanwhile, politicians who in the past had shunned public contacts with bishops began seeking opportunities to hobnob with senior churchmen.

What steps led to the rapprochement between the church and state? Is Salinas's eagerness to extend the olive branch to one of the nation's oldest institutions linked to his effort to modernize what is still a highly statist economy? Will the normalization of relations promote cooperation in social and economic matters, or will a wall of separation spring up between civil and clerical authorities? What are the implications of normalization for several groups—conservative bishops and advocates of liberation theology, for example—within the church? What are the international ramifications of the reconciliation?

These are among the questions addressed in this important study. Unfortunately, little has been written in English about church-state affairs in contemporary Mexico, and most of the accounts in Spanish are brief, journalistic articles. This work by George W. Grayson, a distinguished professor at the College of William and Mary and a preeminent scholar on Mexico, helps fill a conspicuous void. Although focusing on the church, this volume is enriched by the author's wealth of knowledge about Mexico's political system, oil sector, labor movement, and behavior in foreign affairs—all of which have been subjects of previous books by Grayson.

In a carefully organized, meticulously researched, beautifully written study, Grayson explores the history of the Mexican church, examines its origins, discusses the political and social activism of clergy and lay people since the 1960s, and analyzes the events leading to Salinas's decision, announced in his November 1, 1991 state-of-the-nation address, to normalize church-state relations. CSIS is grateful to the Amon G. Carter Foundation for its part in making this study possible.

M. Delal Baer
Director and Senior Fellow
Mexico Project, The Americas Program, CSIS
July 1992

Acknowledgments

For insightful comments on portions of this manuscript, I wish to acknowledge the assistance of M. Delal Baer of the Center for Strategic and International Studies, John J. Bailey of Georgetown University, Roderic Ai Camp of Tulane University, Judith Ewell and James C. Livingston of the College of William and Mary, Carmen Brissette Grayson of Hampton University, Thomas E. Quigley of the U.S. Catholic Conference, Brian H. Smith of Ripon College, and Julie M. Savell, a graduate student at Tulane University. Thanks are due to dozens of members of Mexico's Roman Catholic community for patiently helping an often obtuse foreign scholar understand the church and its activities in their country. I am especially indebted to Father Javier Navarro Rodríguez, executive secretary of the General Secretariat of the Conference of Mexican Bishops, and Licenciado Miguel Ayala Ortiz, adjunct secretary to the Episcopal Commission of Social Communications, for guiding me to documents that aided my study.

Barbara Wright cheerfully and expertly typed the manuscript, and several present and former William and Mary students—Papia Guha, Joan M. Seelaus, Meeta Seghal, and Kristian D. Van Meter—provided research assistance.

With such abundant help, the defects in this volume are obviously my own.

Introduction

The leaders of Mexico and the Soviet Union, like the shah of Iran a decade before, faced an extraordinary challenge in the mid-1980s—namely, how to accomplish sweeping economic reforms without unleashing powerful political forces that could threaten the stability and integrity of their regimes.

Upon taking office in 1985, Mikhail Gorbachev plunged ahead with tandem reforms: *perestroika* to liberalize a closed, inefficient economy and *glasnost* to open an authoritarian, repressive political system. As desirable as both changes were, they gave rise to uncontrollable forces that sparked ubiquitous dissent, chilled production, prompted an abortive coup d'état, scared off many outside investors, made the United States wary of furnishing massive foreign aid, and led to the disintegration of the Soviet Union into the Commonwealth of Independent States.

In contrast, Carlos Salinas de Gortari, president of Mexico, and his predecessor Miguel de la Madrid Hurtado (1982–1988) had the good sense to set priorities. They realized the imperative need to achieve sustained economic growth before creating new channels (and widening others) for releasing the pent-up desires of peasants, blue-collar workers, urban slum dwellers, small businessmen, women, disenchanted elements of the middle class, and other segments of an ever more cynical population.

At first blush, the USSR and Mexico appear so different as to make comparisons between the two seem ludicrous. To begin with, the Soviet Union, with 289 million people before its breakup, had three-and-a-half times the population of Mexico, which has 85 million people. Besides, its landmass was more than 11 times greater than Mexico's.

As in the Soviet Union, a single party, now called the Institutional Revolutionary Party or PRI, has dominated Mexico's political system for more than a half-century. Still, the Mexican political system, in part because of its contiguity to the United States, is infinitely more open and pluralistic than the Rus, Mongol, czarist, and Communist regimes that dominated the USSR for 1,000 years before Gorbachev assumed power. Historically, the Soviets sought to expand their borders, while the Mexicans—traumatized by the loss of half their territory in the Mexican-American War—have concentrated on national integration and development.

These and other differences notwithstanding, striking similarities have characterized the two countries. They include

- bloody revolutions completed early in the century and the persistent trumpeting of the revolutionary mystique,
- large peasant populations beset by poverty and despair,
- massive, pervasive state intrusion into economic affairs,
- sprawling, inefficient bureaucracies whose elites lived sybaritic life-styles, and
- pervasive corruption.

Salinas understood that he, like Gorbachev, had to confront enormously potent vested interests that benefited from a hugely statist economy largely cocooned from external competition by tariffs and import permits. Thus, he moved rapidly to tumble protectionist barriers, privatize state firms, dethrone so-called untouchable labor barons, enhance tax collections, champion capitalism, and launch negotiations for a free-trade accord with the United States and Canada. His reforms bear the sobriquet "Salinastroika"—a play on words based on the *perestroika* advocated by Gorbachev.

Rather than promote two sets of ambitious reforms simultaneously, however, Salinas has emphasized rapid economic modernization complemented by carefully modulated, incremental political change. He understands that plunging headlong toward a freewheeling democracy would excite applause in many circles, including the U.S. Congress, that must approve a North American Free Trade Agreement (NAFTA). Yet pushing a Mexican version of *glasnost* could imperil the bold but fragile economic reforms now under way. Salinas knows that to generate demands that cannot be fulfilled is an invitation to the turmoil and fragmentation that drove Gorbachev from power. Thus he has displayed both a strategy for sustained development and a realistic understanding of the pitfalls inherent in Gorbachev's failure to enlarge the Soviet Union's

economic pie before engendering in its citizens loud, ubiquitous demands for larger slices.

Decisive leadership has lofted Salinas's personal popularity,
but the scope and velocity of his economic initiatives have
alienated and disoriented many people. Among those elements
for which an efficient, modern economy poses the greatest
threat are groups weakly represented or unrepresented by the
authoritarian PRI; specifically, the urban poor, unskilled
workers, owners and employees of small businesses, women,
and old people.

How was Salinas to keep these large, traditional constituen-
cies loyal to the regime as Mexico moved rapidly from an
import-substitution to a market-oriented model of development? To begin with, he renewed a trilateral accord among
labor, business, and the government that helped slash inflation, which had soared to 159.2 percent in 1987, to below 20
percent in 1991. That accord—the Pact for Economic Growth
and Stability (PECE)—has been one of the great success
stories in Latin America in recent years. Declining prices amid
steady, renewed economic growth helped boost workers'
purchasing power, which had been shrinking since the early
1980s. At the same time, the president earmarked billions of
dollars derived from the sale of state firms for a grass-roots
initiative to fight poverty in slums, villages, and the countryside. This National Solidarity Program supports projects selected democratically by local residents who furnish cash,
materials, or "sweat capital" in exchange for government funds
and technical assistance.

Also crucial to bridging the gap between traditional and
modern Mexico has been Salinas's rapprochement with the
Roman Catholic church, long a target of attack by the revolutionary party, labor chiefs, intellectuals, journalists, and leftist
politicians. Although often ignored, provisions of Mexico's
1917 Constitution prohibited the church from owning property, conducting outdoor services, or participating in public
education. Priests could not vote, hold public office, or wear
vestments outside religious buildings. The PRI frequently
rallied militants by warning of "alliances," "secret deals," and
"plots" between bishops and large corporations—especially in

the Monterrey area, which was extremely sensitive to free-enterprise issues. Party demagogues even screamed about a church-Yankee conspiracy when John Gavin, who was then U.S. ambassador to Mexico, lunched with an archbishop and two opposition party leaders in the northern state of Sonora in 1984.

Such attacks by a Tammany Hall-like party viewed as self-serving and corrupt by most Mexicans brightened the image of the church. It won approval for maintaining its financial independence from the government, for the morality of its leaders compared to politicians and bureaucrats, and for its courage in criticizing electoral fraud, wrongdoing by union bosses, and social injustices. Public opinion surveys found that 80 percent of urban Mexicans and 90 percent of rural inhabitants identified themselves as Catholics. Other Mexicans who had little doctrinal attachment to Roman Catholicism expressed their devotion to the Virgin of Guadalupe through medallions swinging from their necks, small statues adorning their automobile dashboards, holy pictures in their homes, and pilgrimages to her shrine in Mexico City.

To overcome the legacy of church-state antagonism, Salinas met with key bishops during his electoral campaign, invited church leaders to his inauguration, dispatched a personal envoy to the Vatican, and exchanged extremely friendly visits with Pope John Paul II. Then, in his 1991 state of the nation address, the president announced plans to amend five articles of the constitution to recognize the church, in fact all churches, as legal entities. His assiduous courting of the church has raised Salinas's approval rating and should attract groups formerly hostile or indifferent to the PRI to the party's nominee in the 1994 presidential election.

This paper traces the history of Mexico's Roman Catholic church, examines its organization and constituent groups, discusses the mounting political and social activism of church leaders in recent years, analyzes Salinas's courtship of Catholic leaders, and speculates on the prospects for church-state relations.

Church and State—A Brief History

During Spain's three centuries of rule in Mexico, the sword and the cross symbolized the pillars of colonial power. Five priests accompanied the aggressively pious Hernán Cortés when he conquered the Aztecs in 1519, and a religious conquest complemented the military subjugation of the Indians. Fresh from expelling the Moors from Iberia and animated by a messianic élan, the Spaniards came to the New World as true believers, convinced that their faith offered the only path to salvation. The missionary priests were determined not only to convert the idol-worshiping, polytheistic Indians to Christianity but also to instruct and civilize them. Especially abhorrent to the Spaniards was the practice of human sacrifice. "It was, perhaps, the last time that Western medieval Christendom attempted to build the City of God here on earth, at the very moment when Europe was turning its back on this particular Utopia in order to pursue others."[1]

Evolution of Catholicism

The number of clergymen soon increased dramatically with the arrival of religious orders and congregations. The Franciscans reached Mexico just four years after Cortés, followed by the Dominicans (1525), Augustinians (1533), and—some time later—the Jesuits (1571). At first, these priests made limited progress in converting the Indians, whose religious outlook—shaped by animism, astrology, sacrifices, and superstition—differed fundamentally from that of Roman Catholicism.[2] Even today, the concept of a universal body of believers is alien to the parochial Indians who often resonate only to the shrine of a saint and the village church.[3]

On December 5, 1531, a miracle occurred that led in the subsequent century to greater acceptance of Catholicism. On that date the Virgin Mary reportedly appeared to a recently converted Indian named Juan Diego. Tradition has it that, in the dazzling moonlight, Diego beheld a serene-eyed, dark-skinned apparition who instructed him to have a shrine built in her honor. This command received all the more acceptance because the figure, who appeared thrice more, presented herself on the hill of Tepeyac, the site in present-day Mexico City where Indians had long worshiped Tonantzin, mother of gods.

Known as "Our Lady of Guadalupe," this manifestation of the virgin has become the so-called Queen of Mexico, the country's patron saint. Each year, she attracts hundreds of thousands of pilgrims, many of whom walk on their knees through the shrine constructed in her honor, tears streaming down their cheeks.

Although Catholicism has not to this day integrated fully with Indian cosmologies, the Virgin of Guadalupe contributed to the accommodation of indigenous and European cultures in what may have been "the greatest missionizing achievement in history."[4] A Franciscan friar, Toribio de Benavente (known as Motolinía), boasted that by 1537 some 9 million Indians had been baptized.[5] In May 1990, Pope John Paul II beatified Juan Diego, whom many Mexican church leaders believe should be elevated to sainthood.

From its arrival in New Spain (as Mexico was then called), the church took a paternalistic interest in the Indians. Juan de Zumárraga, a Franciscan who was bishop of Mexico City, rightfully held the title of "Protector of the Indians" for his efforts to mitigate the hardships suffered by the aboriginal population at the hands of rapacious landholders or *encomenderos*. Bartolomé de las Casas, a Dominican and later bishop of Chiapas, earned even greater fame for his vigorous, militant, and effective advocacy of humane treatment. Such advocacy often brought the church into conflict with government officials and those anxious to enslave and exploit the Indians on large estates, on cattle ranches, and in mines.

Under the authoritarian rule of King Philip II (1556–1598), Madrid became less tolerant of the reform-minded clergy. Meanwhile, with a new generation of churchmen reaching the New World, the church's idealistic impulse to convert and safeguard the natives gave way to a more pessimistic view of their capabilities. They were considered unworthy to enter the priesthood or even to participate in all of the sacraments.

Such pessimism coincided with increased attention by the church, particularly many religious orders and congregations, to the stewardship of its possessions. Its wealth grew, thanks to crown grants, bequests from the faithful, and endowments to churches, monasteries, and nunneries. Ironically, like the landed elite with whom they had found themselves at odds earlier, clerics and religious acquired a powerful stake in Mexico's economic development and political stability. Especially imposing were Jesuit and Franciscan estates, churches, and monasteries, "whose untouchable grandeur controlled half the country."[6] This long-lived coincidence of interest between clerical and lay elites was at the heart of the anticlerical sentiments that periodically blazed forth in the nineteenth century and suffused the 1917 Constitution.

The ever more affluent colonial church was by no means monolithic. At times, bishops linked to the viceroy found themselves at odds with bishops and priests sympathetic to the travail of the Indians. Some diocesan priests, serving under bishops, resented the clergy in religious orders and congregations who were usually better educated and more committed to celibacy and other priestly vows. These different groups of clergy even competed with one another to convert the Indians and to obtain lucrative parishes. Some bishops, members of cathedral chapters, and curates of wealthy parishes boasted annual incomes of 200,000 to 650,000 pesos, while the vast majority received no more than 150 to 300 pesos.[7] The personal bias of the Spanish clergymen, known as peninsular Spaniards, reflected a cleavage that ran through the whole society, for they considered their position to be superior to both their white Mexican-born peers, called Creoles, and to Spanish-Indians, referred to as *mestizos*.

Amid this growing institutional complexity, it was difficult to determine at what point state power gave way to church authority, for the latter was an extension of the former. Through royal patronage (*patronato*), Spanish monarchs exercised considerable control over the Roman Catholic church in their American domains. Thus the king selected bishops whom the pope would automatically approve. Churchmen required the king's permission before traveling to the New

World at royal expense. The church, subsidized and protected by the crown, legitimized decrees issued from Madrid and depended on the viceroys to set and collect tithes. In addition to operating universities, schools, charitable societies, cemeteries, and libraries, the church held mortgages on many estates that it did not own.

Interlocking directorates helped fuse the secular with the religious. For example, Pedro Moya y Contreras, the first inquisitor-general of New Spain, served simultaneously as archbishop and viceroy.[8] Still, as key participants in a corporatist society, church authorities enjoyed exemptions from certain civic obligations and controls. These privileges included freedom from the ordinary administration of justice, thanks to *fueros eclesiásticos,* or special courts, in which clerics sat in judgment on their peers for civil and criminal offenses.

At the behest of the intolerant Philip II, the Mexican church imported the Inquisition in 1571 to preserve the purity of the faith. In addition to denouncing heresy, immorality, and sorcery, this institution, linked to the Holy Office in Rome, examined imported books and newcomers—especially Moors, Jews, and "New Christians" or converts. Civil authorities carried out punishments decreed by the Inquisition. This ecclesiastical body became the crown's most potent weapon against blasphemy, concubinage, and political deviance.

The mushrooming wealth of some religious orders and congregations and their alleged abuse of ecclesiastical lands in Mexico provided the Spanish crown, whose decline was well advanced in Europe by the last third of the seventeenth century, with an excuse to repress their activities. The first order to suffer banishment was the Jesuits, whose 80 estates were confiscated following their expulsion in 1767, an action that was partly attributable to their political involvement in Iberia and elsewhere in Europe. This move brought ruin to their missions, colleges, and apostolates.[9]

Disillusionment in New Spain over the mother country's capricious action sharpened with the 1804 Act of Consolidation. This statute, implemented after the outbreak of war against Great Britain, sequestered the church's charitable monies, diverting some 12 million pesos from pious works in

Mexico to Spanish military adventures in Europe. To pay this forced loan, the church called in notes and mortgages—a move that financially squeezed many members of the landowning elite, thereby alienating them from Madrid.[10] This harsh act was subsequently modified, but it weakened the church and gave impetus to liberal and conservative conspiracies to divorce New Spain from the mother country.[11] In particular, conservative leaders looked askance at Spain's subservience to France—"the symbol, the incarnation, of hateful atheism."[12]

The Church and Independence

Rome strongly opposed Mexico's separation from Spain, but two parish priests who worked among the Indians spearheaded the nineteenth-century independence movement. Miguel Hidalgo y Costilla and José María Morelos incited uprisings against the "tyrannical" Spanish king and his Spanish-born janissaries. Large numbers of downtrodden Indians and *mestizos* flocked to the rebel cause.

The cry of Father Hidalgo epitomized the nationalist sentiment of the movement: "Down with bad government! Death to the *Gachupines* [peninsulars]! Long live religion! Long live our most holy Virgin of Guadalupe!" Hidalgo lofted the banner of the dark Virgin of Guadalupe as the emblem of his movement. Not only did she activate the Indian population, but she also provided a stark contrast to the gold-brocaded Virgin de los Remedios preferred by the Mexican elite.[13] Morelos, in particular, invoked the names of Aztec emperors Montezuma and Cuauhtémoc as he implored his followers to avenge 300 years of exploitation.

Although they achieved notable victories, each curate was eventually captured by loyalist forces, denounced, tried by the Inquisition, defrocked, and shot as a traitor to the motherland. Despite his unrelenting devotion to Roman Catholicism, Hidalgo's persecutors scorned him as "a partisan of French liberty, a libertine, a formal heretic, a Judaiser, a Lutheran, a Calvinist, a rebel, a schismatic, and a suspected atheist."[14]

Ultimately, the independence movement succeeded when the conservative descendants of the Creoles (including high clergymen) joined the opposition to Spain. Their defection was precipitated when King Ferdinand VII swore allegiance to the liberal, democratic Constitution of Cádiz (a product of French influence in Spain) and subsequently attacked the privileges and possessions of the Spanish church.

Senior clerics were eager to halt a sanguinary civil war, accomplish separation from Spain, and protect church property and rights within an independent Mexican state. Thus, they threw their financial and moral support behind Colonel Agustín de Iturbide, military commander of southern Mexico, who proclaimed Mexico's independence in 1821. A year later, the hierarchy took over the *patronato* from the crown, which no longer held sway in Mexico.

The Church and Mexico's Elite

The church emerged from the battles against New Spain possessed of greater organizational coherence, economic wealth, and popular support than the new, fragile Mexican state.[15] To ingratiate himself with the episcopate, Iturbide, whom army garrisons later proclaimed "emperor of Mexico," promised peace based on the Three Guarantees: protection of the Roman Catholic religion and clerical privileges, union, and independence. There were not enough bishops, priests, and religious, however, to take the place of those who had died or returned to Iberia because of their pro-Spanish sentiments. Cathedrals lacked a full complement of clergy, and one-quarter of the 208 convents closed their doors.

Opposition to clerical privileges coalesced around an emerging liberal movement that viewed the Roman Catholic church—because of its affluence, vast landholdings, and conservative outlook—as a bastion of fanaticism and obscurantism that impeded economic development and political reform. Profoundly influenced by the Enlightenment and the French revolution, Mexico's liberals advocated a republican form of government, endorsed individual rights, and favored subordinating the church to civil authority. They also proposed instituting lay education, terminating special military and church courts, selling off church properties to create a nation of small landowners, and clamping a ceiling on sacramental fees exacted from the poor.

Generally sympathetic to these goals were freemasons associated with the anti-Hispanic York rite, introduced by the first U.S. minister to Mexico, Joel Poinsett. This organization competed for members with the pro-Hispanic Scottish rite lodge. Most politicians and even some priests joined the masons, who fostered anticlericalism.

Conservatives and liberals vied for power during most of the period from 1821 to 1876, with the wily General Antonio López de Santa Anna serving as the political arbiter during much of this period. It was during Santa Anna's first presidency that his finance minister, Valentín Gómez Farias, pushed a liberal reform program through Congress. They curbed official support of the church by making tithes voluntary, abolishing civil enforcement of monastic vows, and declaring that the state should control the appointment of bishops. This action led the church to cast its lot with the army, which was outraged by liberal efforts to reduce its size and privileges. Together, the two traditional institutions persuaded Santa Anna to restore conservatives to power and repeal most anticlerical reforms.

In 1836 Pope Gregory XVI recognized the country's independence; his successor named the first apostolic delegate in 1851. As proof of conservative devotion to Mexico's official religion, President José Joaquín Herrera (1848–1851) invited Pope Pius IX, then bedeviled by political travail in Europe, to transfer the Holy See to Mexico.[16]

Liberalism Advances

The ever stronger Liberal Party castigated the church for the political chaos and economic stagnation that characterized Mexico's initial half century of independence. By the 1850s Mexicans had lived under five constitutions, an emperor, and 51 presidents; in addition to war with Texas, they had fought with France and the United States. No wonder that, upon seizing power in the 1855 "Revolution of Ayutla," the Liberals pursued profound changes to replace the discredited institutions of Spanish origin so inextricably bound to authoritarianism and Roman Catholicism. Church lands must be broken up, the reformers averred, to produce a new class of small property holders who would promote stability and order.

The Liberals promulgated the 1857 Constitution, which embraced their ideals, including sweeping controls on the church, now to be separated from the state. Efforts to enforce such provisions on a church that sought to maintain its dominance sparked a bloody, three-year "War of Reform" that ended with a Liberal triumph in 1861.

In the face of this victory, the church welcomed foreign intervention to restore its prerogatives. Its initial support for a French-imposed monarchy tarred the church with the brush of antinationalism. Napoleon III answered the pleas of conservatives by imposing Archduke Maximilian of Austria as emperor of Mexico. Traditionalists argued that only a Catholic monarch would prevent Mexico's national disintegration and absorption by the Protestant, Anglo-Saxon expansionists to the north. The pope proclaimed the 1857 fundamental law to be invalid and backed Maximilian. He also threatened to excommunicate any Mexicans who opposed the French armies.

Maximilian disappointed local ecclesiastical leaders by tolerating other religions and refusing to restore church power completely. When he questioned the wisdom of returning properties expropriated from the Catholic church, the clergy deserted him. The withdrawal of the French troops found him isolated in the nation that he supposedly ruled. The Liberal army captured him and he was executed on the Hill of Bells outside Querétaro in 1867. This act, vehemently opposed by the crowned heads of Europe, to many of whom Maximilian and his wife Carlota were closely related, epitomized Mexican hostility to intervention in the country's affairs.

Liberal presidents Benito Juárez, a Zapotec Indian lawyer from Oaxaca, and Sebastián Lerdo de Tejada, a professor from Veracruz, implemented laws that (1) established complete freedom of worship, (2) declared marriage a civil contract, (3) forbade religious institutions to rent or acquire property, (4) abolished religious oaths in civil acts, (5) banned the public wearing of religious garb, (6) outlawed monastic vows, (7) prohibited religious instruction and worship in public buildings, (8) limited the tolling of church bells to summon the faithful to services, and (9) replaced the swearing of oaths on

Bibles with simple declarations of intent. This program was known as the *Reforma*.

Lerdo also banished from the country the Jesuits (who had been allowed to return in 1853), Sisters of Charity, Passionists, and Vincentians. As one Catholic account observes:

> During those years [of Liberal ascendancy] the Church lost almost all her imposing buildings, which had served as seminaries, colleges, religious houses, or charitable institutions. Almost all the libraries were taken by the government or destroyed. The Church passed through a time of anguish, as did the entire nation, impoverished by wars and discredited before the civilized world. The public treasury was bankrupt, backwardness and poverty were general, and divisions and grudges among the liberal leaders were implacable.[17]

This account exaggerates conditions. Still, the sale of church estates was often to the advantage more of foreign corporations and land speculators than peasants or aspiring middle-class homesteaders. Indeed, the creation of a class of small, yeoman landholders on the French pattern remained a will-o'-the-wisp. The *Reforma* effectively eliminated the church as a source of low-interest loans, while curtailing educational and charitable benefits for large numbers of poor Mexicans.

As part of their economic program, the Liberals invited foreigners to build railroads, establish industries, open mines, cultivate farms, and settle vacant lands. To accommodate the newcomers (many of whom were not Catholic), the government tolerated other religions. With official encouragement, Protestant missionaries from North America entered Mexico to minister to fellow countrymen and other immigrants. This was a period of unprecedented religious tolerance.

Porfiriato (1876–1911)

For pragmatic reasons, General Porfirio Díaz, a former seminarian who began a 35-year dictatorship (known as the *Porfiriato*) in 1876, adopted a conciliatory attitude toward the Roman Catholic church. Although he was the Liberal "hero of

Puebla" in the crucial battle against the French of May 5, 1862, the Machiavellian strongman largely ignored the 1857 Constitution and subsequent anticlerical legislation.

Díaz and his *científico* advisers, who worshiped at the altar of Auguste Comte's positivism and social Darwinism, barred the church from public education. Their intellectual hostility to Roman Catholicism did not blind Díaz's Liberal economic counselors, however, to the functional value of an institution that stressed obedience to authority and the beatitudinal goal of achieving rewards in the afterlife instead of this one.

The president even curtailed anticlericalism practiced by overbearing Liberal governors. "He ruled the country by relying on local leaders who had been, in many instances, as he had been himself, liberal anticlericals in their youth, [but became] church-going autocrats in their middle and old age."[18]

Official benevolence enabled the church to enjoy a renewal, and it regained much of the wealth and influence lost through the Liberal reforms. It expanded the number of ecclesiastical provinces, reopened its own schools and seminaries, invited bishops back from exile, and saw the value of its property double to 100 million pesos. Furthermore, it established religious orders such as those of the reorganized Jesuits, and welcomed the Marists, Salesians, and other religious congregations. New congregations were founded locally, among them the Josephites, the Missionaries of the Holy Spirit, and the Guadalupans.

Most of the hierarchy supported the dictatorial chief executive, whose second wife, Doña Carmen, regularly attended mass. Yet a coterie of progressive priests and lay people worked for social justice in a country where the chasm between "haves" and "have-nots" widened amid the repressive order and uneven economic growth imposed by Díaz.

The ideological momentum for reform sprang from Pope Leo XIII's 1891 encyclical, *Rerum Novarum,* the first great social papal letter and the charter for all subsequent social Catholicism. The pontiff was reacting to the industrial revolution in Europe that had cast so many families into subhuman living and working conditions. He deplored both the excesses of laissez-faire capitalism and the materialist and godless elements of socialism. Although he defended private property as a natural right, he also urged the creation of voluntary groups, including trade unions. These and other mutual aid organizations were to galvanize joint action, overcome worker alienation, and provide a forum for workers and owners to collaborate to improve wages, reduce working hours, and better conditions in the workplace.

The intended result was mutual cooperation rather than Marxist class strife. It was assumed that interclass collaboration and participation would help to empower the oppressed and spark beneficial changes. *Rerum Novarum* thus helped socially concerned Catholicism stage a remarkable recovery by the end of the century. In 1900 the bishop of San Luis Potosí optimistically dismissed the laws of the *Reforma* as "a dead letter."[19]

Influenced by priests who had studied in Europe, progressives convened a series of Catholic Social Congresses: Puebla (1903), Morelia (1904), Guadalajara (1906), and Oaxaca (1909). These conclaves explored how Leo XIII's proposals could be implemented in Mexico. The emphasis was on convincing the political and economic elite of the importance of forming mutual aid societies, not labor unions, to ameliorate conditions in the work place. Also discussed was the need for land reform, housing assistance, protection of child and female labor, profit-sharing programs, social security, savings banks, a minimum wage, and compulsory arbitration in salary disputes.[20]

Revolution and Anticlericalism (1911 to the 1930s)

The hierarchy's close association with Porfirio Díaz contributed to the rabid anticlericalism that was a feature of the revolution that forced the dictator into exile in 1911. That year the church aided in the formation of a National Catholic Party, inspired by the precepts of *Rerum Novarum,* to run legislative candidates in what appeared to be a more open political system.

Any hope that the church would be identified with the nascent democratization was dashed by false rumors that the episcopate had participated in the assassination of the revolution's leader, Francisco Indalecio Madero. The church had, indeed, cast its lot with Victoriano Huerta, the conservative who had overthrown the Madero government. This support, which came in the wake of the episcopate's informal alliance with Díaz, earned the church the enmity of Venustiano Carranza, governor of Coahuila, who was an ardent Madero backer and had spearheaded the anti-Huerta forces as "First Chief of the Constitutionalist Armies."

Upon his victory, Carranza, and the so-called "Northern Jacobins" who had drafted a new fundamental law, took up where Juárez and the nineteenth-century Liberals had left off in terms of anticlericalism. They sought to banish the church from politics, eradicate its social influence, and confine it strictly to religious endeavors. In the constitutional debates, General Francisco Múgica, a vulgar church-baiter, compared the clergy to "vampires" and "vultures."[21]

The language of the new national charter reflected a militant, nationalist, xenophobic spirit that also appeared in music, architecture, and painting. These art forms now depicted ancient native motifs and *mestizo* political struggles. Thus, the anticlerical laws of the nineteenth century were reenacted and even broadened in the often internally contradictory 1917 Constitution, which extolled liberty of thought and conscience even as it repressed expressions of religious beliefs:

- Article 3 decreed that laymen should run schools and prohibited priests from any involvement in elementary education;
- Article 5 forbade the establishment of monastic orders and attacked celibacy and religious vows;
- Article 13 outlawed religious courts;
- Article 24 banned any religious service outside of churches or private homes;
- Article 27 restricted the church from acquiring, possessing, or administering buildings and real estate—with existing and future religious properties declared to be under federal control; in addition, churches and clergy were prevented from owning or operating public or private social welfare institutions; and

- Article 130 declared marriages to be civil contracts; stipulated that the law did not recognize the juridical personality of churches; authorized legislatures to determine the number of priests in the states, all of whom must be born in Mexico; prohibited priests from voting, holding public office, criticizing the constitution, or otherwise participating in politics; set forth strict guidelines for the operation of church buildings; barred religious publications from commenting on national politics; outlawed the formation of confessional parties; and prohibited priests from inheriting property.[22]

After ratification of the nation's new and sweeping charter, governmental authorities largely ignored the document's anticlerical elements. Intent upon achieving hegemony and consolidating their political positions, Presidents Carranza (1917–1920) and Alvaro Obregón (1920–1924) avoided gratuitous fights with Roman Catholics. They treated these provisions as goals of the revolution, not as a reflection of existing social relations. One major exception was Obregón's expulsion in 1923 of Apostolic Delegate Ernesto Filippi for attempting to promote the cult of "Christ, King of Mexico" among the peasants. The chief executive construed such action as seeking to exalt clerical over civil power.[23]

Meanwhile, the church spawned a network of lay-oriented organizations to protect itself against the anticlerical provisions of the constitution. Among the most important groups were the National Parents' Union, formed in 1917 to promote parochial education, and the Social Secretariat, established in 1919 to advance the Catholic reform ideology that had appeared late in the Porfirian era. In turn, the Social Secretariat created organizations for women, peasants, and workers. By 1922 the Catholic National Federation of Labor was rapidly adding workers to its existing 80,000 members. These advances raised the hackles of the power-hungry Luis Morones, head of the pro-Obregón Regional Confederation of Mexican Workers (CROM). Later, these Catholic groups formed part of the Catholic Action movement championed by Pope Pius XI, which is described in chapter 2.[24]

Cristero Uprising (1926–1929)

It remained for President Plutarco Elías Calles (1924–1928), who as a child had pilfered coins from the alms box to buy candy, to implement the constitution's provisos against the church with a vengeance. His action came after a Mexico City newspaper had published a letter written by Archbishop José Mora y del Río. This letter denounced anticlericalism in certain states and declared that Roman Catholics could not in good conscience accept the constitution. Even though the outdated document no longer reflected the church's current, accommodationist policy toward the government, Calles seized upon it to consolidate the autonomy of the state.

The chief executive regarded the church as a political enemy whose defeat was crucial to preserving the revolutionary regime. He banished foreign priests, nuns, and many bishops who had come to "fanaticize" the people. He ordered the jailing of other priests and religious brothers and sisters, while Mexican clergy were forced to register with civil authorities. In addition, his government outlawed religious processions, confiscated those church properties not yet nationalized, and suppressed convents, monasteries, and parochial schools. Calles also acquiesced in an initiative by Morones, aided by two defrocked priests, to establish a schismatic Orthodox Catholic Apostolic Church. This divide-and-conquer tactic, popular in Mexico, was employed to siphon believers away from traditional Roman Catholicism.

Ironically, in response to what seemed like another *Kulturkampf* (a cultural crusade), Mora y del Río employed Liberal rhetoric to champion individual freedom and political independence. To combat the oppressive state, he declared a strike that lasted three years. During this period, no masses were celebrated, no babies baptized, no confessions heard, and no last rites administered—except clandestinely or for the wealthy who sometimes paid priests to dispense the sacraments.

Infuriated by Calles's crudely abusive attack on their faith and rights, zealous Catholics in western and north-central states, the heartland of the religion, rose up against the blasphemers in Mexico City. At the forefront of this movement was the Federation for the Defense of Religious Liberty. Many of the rebels were peasants who sought land promised, but not provided, by the revolutionary regime.

The Vatican inveighed against Calles's action. In a November 1926 encyclical, *Iniquis Afflictique,* Pope Pius XI reviewed and protested the suppression of Mexican Catholics, expressed solidarity with clergy and laymen, and contended that "in no place or at no time has it happened before that a small group of men has so outraged the rights of God and of the Church as they are now doing in Mexico."[25]

This *Cristero* movement, whose name derived from the rallying cry of "¡Viva Cristo Rey!" launched a guerrilla war. It burned schools, murdered teachers, and even bombed a train running between Mexico City and Guadalajara, killing more than 100 people. Even though only a handful of the country's 3,600 priests had taken up arms, the government struck back with fury as soldiers pledged to kill a priest for every dead teacher.[26] In his novel *The Power and the Glory,* Graham Greene captures the mood of persecution as the governor of Tabasco inexorably hounds Padre José and other priests. All told, the violence, sharpened by the 1928 assassination of Obregón by a religious extremist, consumed 250,000 to 300,000 lives, many of whom were Catholics killed after a compromise was hammered out.

In mid-1929, a bargain was struck following months of negotiations that involved the American ambassador, Dwight Morrow, President Emilio Portes Gil, head of the provisional government, and the new apostolic delegate, Archbishop Leopoldo Ruiz y Flores. The chief executive pledged to allow the Catholic hierarchy to designate those priests required to register in compliance with national laws. In addition, he agreed not to interfere with religious instruction conducted within places of worship and to permit the clergy, like other Mexican citizens, to seek modification of the constitution.

Although they denied any involvement in the rebellion, the hierarchy repudiated violence and commanded the *Cristeros* to halt operations and the clergy to reopen the churches. In a pastoral letter, Ruiz y Flores urged all priests to avoid political involvement and laymen to obey the nation's laws: "We have offered to cooperate with the government with all our resources, moral and otherwise, for the betterment of the people," stated the directive.[27]

The pealing of church bells greeted the signing of the 1929 accord between Portes Gil and Ruiz y Flores, as priests gradually reclaimed sanctuaries from neighborhood committees appointed by the civil authority. Following the ceremony, the apostolic delegate and the Mexican bishops drove directly to the shrine of the Virgin of Guadalupe, where they knelt in prayer for 10 minutes. Meanwhile, the Southern Pacific Railway furnished a free Pullman train to bring expatriate prelates back from San Antonio to Mexico City. A government ministry dispatched a steamer to the prison colony on the islands of Las Tres Marías to retrieve black-swathed, pious women incarcerated for defying the law by practicing their religion.[28]

Renewed Anticlericalism (1930s)

This reconciliation aside, the "revolutionary party," founded in 1929 and today called the PRI, made the church, along with big business and Yankee imperialism, one of its favorite scapegoats in subsequent years. "The position of the state toward the private sector . . . [in the 1917 Constitution] is contradictory, but its posture toward the Church is quite clear. Mexico's political elites, for reasons of ideology and the desire to monopolize the state apparatus, curtailed and attacked the Catholic Church's political activities."[29] Amid the cheers of his fellows, a delegate from Tabasco at a party convention in 1933 expressed the views of many official party militants when he screamed: "There is no God. We should forget God and the clergy. God exists only in petrified souls. The Mexican revolution wants no God and the revolutionary party wants no God." The convention ended with the delegates shouting: "Down with God! Down with the church!"[30]

Such sentiments help to explain the hostile acts against the church that continued throughout the 1930s, although with somewhat less frequency than before. On December 12, 1931, demonstrators cursed and pummeled the faithful who celebrated the 400th anniversary of the appearance of the Virgin of Guadalupe. Detractors ridiculed this event as a "heathenish feast" and "vulgar farce." General Calles, who as war secretary still served as the nation's *jefe máximo* (supreme leader), discharged from military service 80 musicians of an army band that played at the Guadalupe basilica without his approval.[31]

Postrevolutionary federal and state statutes bristled with anticlericalism. The national government refused to recognize credits earned by students attending religious secondary schools. The regime authorized only 24 priests for the 1 million Catholics in the Federal District, only 200 of whose several thousand churches could be used for religious purposes; the Congress permitted no clerics in Quintana Roo, then a territory; the state legislature decreed that there should be no more than one priest for every 100,000 inhabitants in Veracruz, where Cortés had first set foot on Mexican soil; and only married clerics could discharge their priestly functions in Tabasco. So rabid was the anticlericalism in this southeastern state that pictures of nude priests adorned the walls of the local union headquarters, and many concurred in the saying: "God is not officially permitted in Tabasco." Mounting attacks on seminaries forced the Vatican to open a seminary for Mexican candidates for the priesthood in Montezuma, New Mexico.

On September 30, 1932, Pope Pius XI responded to such restrictions with the encyclical *Acerba Animi*. In this Vatican letter, he expressed deep compassion for his Mexican brethren, praised the fortitude shown by clergy and laymen in the face of "iniquitous," "impious," and "pernicious" laws, and compared the "wicked persecution" in Mexico to that which reigned in Russia. Still, he counseled Mexicans to obey the laws formally even as they protested their validity. The pope stated that

> we join our protests to yours before the whole world and in a special manner before the Rulers of the Nations, to make them realize that the persecution of Mexico, besides being an outrage against God, against His Church, and against the conscience of a Catholic people, is also an incentive to the subversion of the social order, which is the aim of those organizations professing to deny God.[32]

The pontiff urged priests to spurn illegal actions in favor of rendering "even more intense their sacred ministry," especially among the young and common people. He emphasized the imperative of persuasion and charity vis-à-vis enemies of the church, while giving even greater impetus to Catholic Action.[33]

Abelardo Rodríguez, the third puppet president manipulated by Calles after Obregón's death, greeted the papal letter as the political equivalent of chewing glass shards: "I am resolved," he said, "that if this vulgar and defiant attitude is continued . . . the churches shall be converted into schools and factories for the benefit of the proletarian classes of Mexico." The Chamber of Deputies followed suit by approving a resolution to deport Apostolic Delegate Ruiz y Flores.[34]

In mid-October 1932, the legislators voted to banish all bishops after Archbishop Pascual Díaz publicly opposed an education reform. Specifically, the new law decreed that Marxism, socialism, and atheism, as well as sex education, must be taught in the public schools. President Rodríguez immediately ordered the attorney general to investigate "subversive activities" carried out by members of the clergy and other "Catholic reactionaries" who were of "doubtful Mexican nationality."[35]

Church-State Reconciliation (Late 1930s)

Lázaro Cárdenas, who assumed the presidency in late 1934, called a truce to the church-state squabbling. No friend of Roman Catholicism—he criticized the church for having "delayed the nation's social and economic evolution"—the new president ordered all schools to teach socialism, Marxism, atheism, and sex education.[36] Still, he had higher priorities than persecuting the clergy. The former governor of Michoacán was fond of saying that he was "tired of closing churches and finding them full." He would have preferred to open them and "find them empty."[37]

He had to seize the reins of authority from the power-crazed Calles, who—before being drummed into exile—attempted to treat Cárdenas like a mere lackey. In addition, Cárdenas sought to implement the social provisions of the constitution by distributing farm land to peasants, encouraging the organization of new unions, and nationalizing the railroads, oil industry, and other sectors of the economy. Ironically, Cárdenas's sympathy with the plight of the dispossessed earned him the sobriquet of "Tata Lázaro," recalling the beloved sixteenth-century bishop of Michoacán, "Tata" Vasco de Quiroga.[38]

Cárdenas also wanted to make the official party more responsive to the chief executive. To this end, he drew upon the corporatist tradition, rooted in the philosophy of St. Thomas Aquinas, in revamping the revolutionary party. He replaced a hierarchical structure with one dominated by four functional groupings: peasant, labor, white collar/professional, and military (dissolved in 1940). These sectors, it was argued, would promote order and harmony among the diverse elements in Mexican society. They also enhanced hierarchical control, a hallmark of the nation's political system.

To propitiate the church, Cárdenas prevailed upon the state legislature to repeal the law preventing religious ceremonies in Veracruz. The Mexican Supreme Court, extremely sensitive to executive wishes, declared unconstitutional a Chihuahua law that permitted only one priest in the entire state. And "Godless Tabasco," now in the hands of a Cárdenas-approved governor, adopted a more conciliatory attitude toward Roman Catholics.

The aged and ailing Pope Pius XI recognized the changes in his Easter letter to the Mexican bishops in 1937. He appealed for church unity, urged the episcopate to raise the clergy's educational standards, and called for spiritual and material assistance to industrial and agricultural workers as well as the promotion of justice and charity "to assure all that minimum of this world's goods that is indispensable to safeguard human dignity and eliminate abuses."[39] These words had the ring of a Cárdenas speech.

Even more pleasing to the president was the pronouncement of Archbishop Luis M. Altamirano y Bulnes, secretary of the Episcopal Committee, who implored "Mexican Catholics to contribute generously to the government . . . to pay the debt contracted with regard to the nationalization of petroleum companies." He went on to say that "the episcopal committee . . . declares not only can Catholics contribute to the end expressed in the manner deemed opportune, but that this contribution will be an eloquent testimonial that Catholic doctrine is a stimulus to carrying out citizenship duties and gives solid base to true patriotism."[40] Thus, the church, which had defiantly set its face against the nationalistic and revolutionary currents so evident early in the century, had executed a turnabout: now it identified itself fully with the chief executive who was attempting to implement the social doctrine embedded in the 1917 Constitution, a document that had once been so loathsome to the bishops.

The church's official position notwithstanding, many Catholics decried Cárdenas as an architect of socialism who was intent upon converting Mexico into a Spanish-speaking Soviet Union. Some right-wing, former *Cristeros* who held this belief organized the National Sinarchist Union (UNS) in León, Guanajuato, in 1937. Sympathetic to Spain's Francisco Franco, Portugal's António Salazar, and Brazil's Getulio Vargas, these Catholics sought to preserve the central tenets of Catholic civilization against atheistic, leveling Marxism. The *sinarquistas* condemned gringos along with Bolsheviks as purveyors of the materialist, Godless values that they reviled: "Soviet Communism and North American capitalism are manifestations of the same revolution . . . whose physical presence is to be found in fanatical Judaism and whose fruits sprang from the French, Mexican, and Russian Revolutions."[41] Although led by middle-class activists, the *sinarquistas* appealed chiefly to peasants who remained landless and poor despite the revolution.

The UNS claimed 1 million members at the outbreak of World War II, when it enthusiastically backed Hitler. "Ultrareactionary leaders stressed their hatred of Communism, openly disparaged the [Liberal] Reforma and the Revolution, but lauded the glories of Mexico under the Hapsburgs, when Church and State were coordinate arms of Catholicism."[42] To prevent UNS fifth-column subversion, the government enacted the Espionage Law of 1941. Despite some ugly riots, this law combined with the official party's skillful use of infiltration, patronage, and intimidation broke the back of *sinarquismo*. The movement's latter-day manifestation, the Mexican Democratic Party (PDM), has never obtained more than 3 percent of the national vote.[43]

More moderate critics of *Cardenismo* organized the National Action Party (PAN). Created in 1939, the new party drew its inspiration from papal encyclicals. Manuel Gómez Morín, a distinguished intellectual who founded the party and served as its first president, was determined that Catholic values survive in an increasingly secular world. He favored revising the 1917 Constitution to guarantee religious freedom, joined church leaders in opposing socialist education, championed private enterprise, and urged modifying the agrarian reform to substitute individual holdings for those held by the traditional Indian communities know as *ejidos*. In view of the ever present threat of official suppression, the PAN declared itself nonconfessional. Still, the party attracted many Catholic activists and its name bore a striking similarity to that of Catholic Action.[44] Its name also conjured memories of the right-wing *Action Française,* although the PAN spurned the anti-Semitic and pro-monarchical tendencies of the French organization.[45]

Collaboration (1940–1958)

Cárdenas's hand-picked candidate, General Manuel Avila Camacho, defeated a wealthy, right-wing Catholic to win the presidency in 1940. During his electoral campaign, he had declared, apparently to please his mother, that "I believe in God."[46] As part of an effort to make peace with foes of the revolution, Avila Camacho ushered in three decades of collaboration between church and state. Mexico City's archbishop, Luis María Martínez, asked all Catholics to support the new chief executive, with whom he enjoyed an especially good rapport.

Except for softening provisions of Article 3 offensive to the church, Avila Camacho did not alter the constitution. Yet, he and the Roman Catholic leadership worked out an informal truce, subject to ad hoc rules, much like those that characterized the Porfirian era. For its part, the government would ignore (but not repeal) the fundamental law's draconian strictures, provided that the hierarchy agreed to stay out of politics. "Leaders on both sides recognized that neither could probably win an open contest of national proportions, or rather, that winning would not be worth the cost."[47]

In general, flourishing lay organizations, while eschewing most social struggles, acted as church surrogates in such narrow political areas as education and social morality. Moreover, the new rules ensured behind-the-scenes negotiations on controversial subjects of mutual interest. Such parleys helped confine disputes to local brushfires rather than allowing them to blaze into nationwide conflagrations. Above all, the church diminished its social militancy: Catholic-inspired trade unions and the Catholic Action movement atrophied. Increasingly, ecclesiastical authorities perceived the official party, with all of its warts and blemishes, as a known quantity that represented stability. To weaken the keystone in the revolutionary system might produce both its fall and the advent of chaos and raw anticlericalism that would menace the institutions of the church and its adherents.

Under the umbrella of this modus vivendi, church-state relations improved notably. Seminaries reopened, the number of priests and religious grew, and the church's role in education expanded. Thus, by 1975 some three-fourths of the 1,400 priests in the Mexico City archdiocese were foreign missionaries who went about their labors free from harassment by civil authorities.[48] Priests obtained passports by identifying themselves as "school teachers" on application forms. And, although Article 27 forbade the church to own real estate, wealthy Catholics, associations, or corporations could purchase any properties they wanted.[49] In some Catholic schools, a fast-talking nun would delay an education inspector at the door while other teachers turned a framed religious image to the wall, displaying the stern countenance of Benito Juárez on the other side.[50]

Contributing to the warmer atmosphere was the urging of Martínez, who also served as apostolic delegate, that the faithful back Mexico's decision, taken in May 1942, to declare war on the Axis powers. Later in the year, Martínez stated that "it is a sin for Catholics not to cooperate with the government." Avila Camacho praised the prelates for helping "greatly in unifying the country and strengthening morale."[51]

The 1946 presidential election proved an acid test for the "new era" in church-state relations. Since the formation of the revolutionary party in 1929, opponents of its candidates typically arose from the party itself—often unsuccessful aspirants for the nomination. In the 1946 contest, the revolutionary party's nominee, Miguel Alemán, faced a challenge from a different quarter: the National Action Party. Eager to nurture their collaborative relationship with the official party, Archbishop Martínez admonished the clergy to abstain from political activity in the 1946 presidential election. Many priests ignored this counsel and joined Catholic laymen in backing the PAN's nominee, Ezequiel Padilla, whom Alemán trounced. Still, the archbishop of Mexico City physically embraced Alemán, symbolizing how much church-state affairs had improved in little more than a decade.

This post-1940 reconciliation continued in 1952 when Adolfo Ruiz Cortines, the revolutionary party's standard-bearer, affixed his signature to a widely distributed campaign poster that read: "Religion of the People IS Sacred."[52] In the same spirit, Ruiz Cortines's successor, Adolfo López Mateos, proclaimed: "There exists in Mexico absolute freedom of belief. The ample program of the revolution can encompass all men of good will."[53]

Just as church and state had joined forces against the Axis powers during World War II, both institutions staunchly opposed the spread of Soviet influence in the postwar years. "In that period the ecclesiastical hierarchy was stressing that both the political and religious powers had the same mission in Mexico: to preserve and promote national culture against external attack, which in those years basically meant international communism."[54] This ideological convergence found Catholic leaders helping to legitimize a regime that, in appreciation for its backing, permitted the church greater freedom of action.

During López Mateos's *sexenio* (1958–1964), new issues joined education to strain future relations between clergy and politicians. Never, however, did the disputes generate the violence and repression witnessed before 1940. An examination of the church's internal structure provides insights into the conditions that inspired renewed social activism on the part of Mexico's Roman Catholic hierarchy in the 1960s.

Figure 1
Diagram of the Conference of Mexican Bishops (CEM)

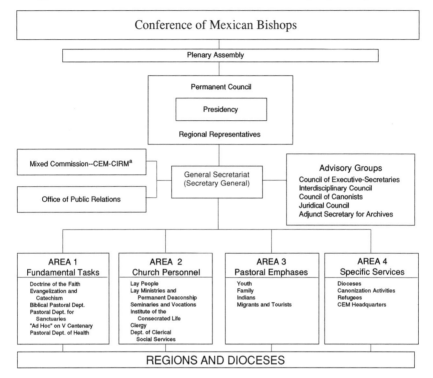

Source: Conferencia del Episcopado Mexicano, *Directorio 1989–1991* (Mexico City: CEM, 1990).

[a]Conference of Religious Institutes of Mexico.

2
Organization of Mexico's Roman Catholic Church

The organizational chart of Mexico's Roman Catholic church, like its counterparts in other countries, resembles a flat-topped Aztec temple (see figure 1). A succession of bodies has occupied the top of this structure. Between 1935 and 1937, the Mexican Episcopal Executive Committee served as the unifying body of the Mexican church and as its official organ for disseminating and defending the faith. Beginning in 1937, this role was played by the Mexican Bishops' Committee. In October 1953, the Committee was replaced by the far less authoritarian and hierarchical Conference of Mexican Bishops (CEM), which was founded in response to Pope Pius XII's proposal for the creation of episcopal conferences in each country to integrate the spiritual and political work of the hierarchy.

The conference, which includes all bishops and which functions collegially, pursues solutions to problems related to pastoral duties; seeks unity of goals and action in advancing appropriate apostolic strategies; and determines the most efficient and suitable means for priests, deacons, religious, and laymen to fulfill the church's unique mission of salvation.[1] Its Plenary Assembly, which meets each spring and fall, constitutes the CEM's most influential policy-making organ. Active bishops and bishops emeriti may participate in the assembly: the former with voice and vote, the latter with voice only.[2]

When appropriate, assembly organizers ask priests, laymen, and foreign clergy to prepare a paper or speak on a specific topic. The invitation defines the guest's scope of involvement in the assembly. Traditionally, organizers have invited the apostolic delegate to address the opening session and to attend the other sessions. Recent assemblies have focused on such topics as planning and evaluating pastoral work, the church's role in education, church-state relations, lay ministries, and new religious groups (a euphemism for Protestant missionaries and evangelical sects). The special July

1990 Plenary Assembly, attended by 93 bishops, considered the significance and consequences for their country of Pope John Paul II's recent visit to Mexico.

Perhaps the most important function discharged by the assembly is selecting the CEM officers. In preparing for an election, the secretary general, whose other tasks are described below, solicits proposals from the 15 pastoral regions for candidates to become part of the six-man Presidency. From these suggestions, he submits to the Permanent Council a list of names, as well as the degree of support enjoyed by each nominee. The Permanent Council acts as a kind of nominating committee for the assembly in preparing a list of candidates for president. Of course, any active bishop may make a nomination from the floor inasmuch as assemblies are open and freewheeling forums receptive to a wide spectrum of viewpoints.

The six-man Presidency is the main executive organ of the conference and its Permanent Council. The members of the six-man Presidency, who may serve two consecutive three-year terms, are the president, vice president, secretary general, and treasurer of the CEM, as well as two spokesmen elected from the pastoral regions.[3] The functions of the president of the conference are to (1) represent the CEM juridically, (2) convoke the Plenary Assembly, (3) oversee deliberations of the Permanent Council and preside over it, (4) make extraordinary decisions in key cases, and (5) approve, in concert with other members of the Presidency, the exceptional economic activities of the CEM.[4] Archbishop Adolfo Suárez Rivera of Monterrey, who was elected president of the conference in November 1988, exhibits both the formal and informal qualities of the six men who have held this position since the CEM's creation. The statutes require that the president be a bishop, but in fact only archbishops have filled this post. Moreover, the Vatican has recommended that ordinaries, not auxiliary bishops, serve as president. Informal requirements of presidents include being middle-aged, possessing diplomatic skills, exhibiting a moderate political posture, and presiding in an important (Mexico City, Puebla, and Guadalajara) or reasonably important (Oaxaca, Jalapa, Monterrey) archdiocese. (See table 1.)

Table 1
Presidents of the Conference of Mexican Bishops (CEM)

Name	Date of Birth	Archdiocese at Time of Appointment	Period in Office
Mons. José Garibi Rivera Archbishop of Guadalajara	January 30, 1889	Guadalajara	1942–1953,[a] 1958–1963
Mons. Octaviano Márquez y Toriz Archbishop of Puebla	March 22, 1904	Puebla	1953–1958, October 1963– February 1968
Mons. Ernesto Corripio Ahumada Archbishop of Oaxaca	June 29, 1919	Oaxaca	February 1968– October 1973
Cardinal José Salazar López Archbishop of Guadalajara	January 12, 1910	Guadalajara	October 1973– December 1979
Mons. Ernesto Corripio Ahumada Archbishop of Puebla	June 29, 1919	Mexico City	December 1979– November 1982
Mons. Sergio Obeso Rivera Archbishop of Jalapa	October 31, 1931	Jalapa	November 1982– November 1988
Mons. Adolfo A. Suárez Rivera Archbishop of Monterrey	January 9, 1927	Monterrey	November 1988– Present

Source: Father Javier Navarro Rodríguez, executive secretary to CEM's secretary general. Interviews, June 15, 1990, and August 31, 1990.

[a]During this period, Garibi Rivera presided over the Mexican Bishops' Committee, predecessor to the CEM.

The president works closely with his fellow members on the 21-member Permanent Council. Constituted by the Presidency and representatives from the 15 pastoral regions, the Permanent Council is responsible for ensuring the implementation and continuity of CEM objectives. As the "representative organ" of the bishops, this Council meets quarterly, although the CEM president or an absolute majority of its members may call a special session at any time.[5]

A General Secretariat carries out the conference's day-to-day activities of coordination, communication, and disseminating information. The secretariat, which also plans the Plenary Assemblies, is composed of a secretary general and one or more assistant secretaries. CEM's statutes declare a preference that the bishop selected as secretary general have no other duties.[6]

Various bodies assist the General Secretariat in discharging its functions: a mixed commission of regular and secular clergy (Mixed Commission of the Conference of Mexican Bishops and the Conference of Religious Institutes of Mexico [CEM-CIRM]), a Public Relations Office, four advisory groups (Executive Secretaries, Interdisciplinary, Canonical, and Judicial), and an archivist. A bishop heads each of the four areas of church activities: (1) Fundamental Tasks, (2) Church Personnel, (3) Pastoral Emphases, and (4) Specific Services.[7]

At the base of Mexico's church lie the 15 pastoral regions comprising 71 archdioceses and dioceses, which—in turn—are broken down into 4,802 parishes. At the beginning of 1990, 8,090 of the nation's 11,317 priests were diocesan and 3,227 were religious.[8] Two years earlier, the church had boasted 24,819 sisters, 1,306 religious brothers, and 5,253 seminarians.[9]

Regional Groupings of Bishops

History, geography, and economic factors often influence the behavior of bishops in various parts of the country. Traditionally, members of the episcopate in the Mexico City-Puebla-Guadalajara arc have been associated with the church's moderate or "historic" current that deals with the government. Adding to the area's importance is the fact that it embraces two cardinal sees, Mexico City and Guadalajara. Under canon

law, cardinals have responsibility only for their archdioceses.
Mexico City, however, is the administrative hub of a highly
centralized country, and its cardinal is expected to interest
himself in national questions. The concentration of the federal
bureaucracy and industry in the capital means that, over the
years, cardinals and bishops from Mexico City have found
themselves negotiating with government and business leaders
on issues as varied as birth control, human rights, and clerical
privileges. Further enhancing the central bishops' role as
political interlocutors is the presence, in Mexico City, of the
apostolic delegate, the Vatican's representative to the Mexican
bishops.

Characteristics of the North shape the behavior of many
local bishops there as well. States in this area enjoy relatively
advanced economic development, favor market-focused policies (with Monterrey serving as the mecca of free enterprise),
lie close to the United States with which their economies are
intertwined, and boast the presence of the strongest opposition
party, the pro-Catholic, business-oriented National Action
Party. Northern churchmen have often cooperated enthusiastically with the PAN, while enjoying overt ties to the local
business community. As discussed below, these prelates
assumed an extremely high profile in the 1980s when they
excoriated scandals in state and local elections.

Less concerned with negotiations at the federal level,
northern bishops have developed competences relevant to
their region. A case in point is Emilio Carlos Berlie Belaunzarán,
bishop of Tijuana, who heads the Episcopal Commission for
Ministering to Migrants and Tourists. Similarly, Manuel
Talamás Camandari, bishop of Ciudad Juárez, specializes in
the needs of workers in the 1,936 *maquiladora* twin-assembly
plants concentrated along the U.S. border.

Compared to the central and northern regions, the South
appears as a distinct country, resembling Central America
more than the rest of Mexico. This violence-prone area over-
flows with impoverished peasants, powerless Indians, Guatemalan refugees, intimidating landlords, and exploitative
political bosses. These conditions have contributed to the
acceptance of liberation theology by a half-dozen southern
bishops.

Liberation Theology

The body of religious thought known as liberation theology, first articulated by the Peruvian priest Gustavo Gutiérrez in the early 1970s, shifts the emphasis of religious faith from salvation in heaven to liberation on earth and promotes *comunidades eclesiales de base* (CEBs). Usually, these base communities are small, lay-led groups of mostly poor people, who combine Bible study with consciousness-raising about their abject conditions. Their scripture study may catalyze both mutual help and political action in defense of their rights.[10] In addition, liberation theology deplores the evils of capitalism, emphasizes Christ's role as a social revolutionary, and stakes out an explicit position on behalf of the "have-nots" as opposed to the "haves."[11]

Sergio Méndez Arceo, who died in early 1992, was this faction's outspoken and undisputed leader until his retirement in 1982 at age 75. Cuernavaca's feisty "Red Bishop" unabashedly supported Fidel Castro, backed the Sandinistas in Nicaragua, demanded that inequalities in Mexico's socioeconomic order be redressed, lambasted U.S. imperialism, and promoted a dialogue between Christians and Marxists. His energetic enthusiasm for Marxist movements earned Méndez Arceo rebukes from both the CEM hierarchy and the Vatican: the former in a March 9, 1978, declaration; the latter in the failure of Pope John Paul II to send him the customary letter of congratulations when he completed 25 years as bishop. In recent years, Méndez Arceo's mantle has passed to Bishop Samuel Ruiz García of San Cristóbal de las Casas in the South, who has emerged as Mexico's most visible and persistent advocate of liberation theology.

Still, the beliefs espoused by Gutiérrez and advanced by Méndez Arceo and Ruiz have failed to win broad acceptance within the hierarchy. The church in Mexico lacks an ideological doctrine molded to national circumstances. Indeed, "the country possesses no solid theological tradition of praxis, of 'reading the signs of the times' or of interpreting Mexican secular reality in ways analogous to what is found in Brazil with Leonardo Boff, in Peru with Gustavo Gutiérrez, or in Uruguay with Juan Luis Segundo."[12]

The several Mexico City research centers that pursue liberationist themes—the Centro de Reflexión Teológica (Jesuit), the Centro de Derechos Humanos M. A. Pro (Jesuit), the Centro de Estudios Dominicanos (Dominican), and the Centro Antonio de Montecinos (lay)—have limited influence in the upper reaches of the clergy.[13] Yet these "think tanks," and magazines such as *Christus* and *Cencos,* provide ideological nourishment to tens, perhaps hundreds, of thousands of lay people, priests, religious brothers and sisters who subscribe to liberationist values. Enhancing the attraction of these values is the grinding poverty and political impotence that is the lot of more than one-third of Mexicans.

In addition to the southern states of Chiapas and Oaxaca, these progressives are found in the greatest numbers in Mexico City, Chihuahua, Veracruz, and Morelos. According to one of the movement's intellectual leaders, the early 1990s found progressive Mexican Catholics undergoing a period of "consolidation" characterized by "greater balance, greater clarity, and greater patience."[14]

The most serious confrontation between liberationists and the hierarchy occurred in 1989 as part of a regional face-off. In the late 1980s, the Latin American Conference of Religious (CLAR), a federation of various orders and congregations composed of 160,000 men and women religious of the continent and committed to the "preferential option for the poor," embarked upon a project to celebrate the fifth century of New World missionary activity. Termed the "Plan Palabra-Vida" (Word-Life Plan), the program anticipated the publication of five pamphlets, the first of which was entitled *La palabra convoca.* Both the Latin American Episcopal Conference (CELAM) and CEM found this "disgusting" document to be "reductionist" and suffused with "the Marxist version" of liberation theology to the possible point of "heresy." A passage particularly objectionable to the hierarchy stated that "The greatest certainty that the Bible communicates is this: God hears the clamor of oppressed people. He is present in the life and the struggle of these people and helps their liberation."[15]

CLAR complied with CELAM's insistence that the "Plan Palabra-Vida" be modified, including the recall and revision of the offending pamphlet. A local version of this controversy found the CEM voicing its objections to the program to CLAR's Mexican affiliate, the Conference of Religious Institutes of Mexico, which also agreed to the modifications. Such submission aside, Mexico's religious orders and congregations still embrace a disproportionate number of advocates of liberation theology.[16]

Clerics of different theological orientations remain on cordial personal terms, even though Bishop Ruiz's outspokenness sometimes vexes his moderate colleagues. Arturo Lona Reyes, bishop of Tehuantepec and another staunch advocate of liberation theology, serves as a bridge between Ruiz and the centrists.[17]

Rome's Influence

The Vatican exercises enormous influence over the Mexican church. As many as half the bishops were at least quietly sympathetic to liberation theology before Pope John Paul II's trip to the country in 1979. The pontiff persuaded the vast majority of bishops to spurn a doctrine grounded in militant activism for the poor and, instead, to emphasize the church's evangelical role and the traditional morality of the common good. His success sprang from both his 1979 exhortation and his subsequent appointment of more conservative prelates. A cartoonist captured this change when he depicted Cardinal Ernesto Corripio Ahumada and two priests waving good-bye to the pope; on the ground behind them lay a bruised and battered priest, clutching a banner adorned with the words, "Liberation Theology."[18]

Eleven years later, the bishops were divided on the proper strategy to follow in response to President Salinas's overtures for closer church-state relations. Specifically, should they insist on extensive revision of Article 130 and other juridical concessions as a precondition to rapprochement? Or, might pragmatic moves—for example, avoiding any offense to the government in hopes that it would undertake diplomatic relations with the Vatican—suffice until the climate favored revamping the fundamental law?

Confidential church sources reported that key bishops, led by CEM president Suárez Rivera and his legal adviser, Luis

Reynoso Cervantes, bishop of Cuernavaca, endorsed constitutional changes as a sine qua non for improved relations. A
substantial majority, including Bishop Hilario Chávez Joya,
prelate of Nuevo Casas Grandes, would have preferred to
remain silent because of inertia, absorption in pastoral tasks,
or inexperience in nonpartisan, pastoral politics.[19] By the time
the pope left Mexico City in May 1990, virtually all of the
bishops had coalesced behind Suárez Rivera and Reynoso
Cervantes.

Several factors explain the Holy See's influence in Mexico,
which is markedly greater than that exerted on bishops in the
United States or Brazil. First, the Mexican church feels a debt
to the Vatican for bestowing unflinching support during Roman
Catholicism's darkest days in its country—namely, the revolution, the Calles repression, and the *Cristero* uprising. Clerics
still praise the compassion, support, and sensitivity exempli-
fied by Pius XI's 1926 and 1932 encyclicals to Mexican Catholics. Second, Mexico's political culture emphasizes discipline
and obedience to authority. Just as mayors, governors, and
cabinet secretaries exhibit these traits in relations with the
president, bishops seem particularly submissive to the pope.[20]
Third, in recent years, CEM presidents and the irascible, tired
Corripio have provided relatively weak leadership. Thus, the
Vatican has filled the void. Fourth, as in other nations, since
1978 Pope John Paul II has selected conservative bishops who
are likely to defend Rome's theological and political positions.
Finally, the current apostolic delegate, Jerónimo Prigione, is
intelligent, shrewd, gregarious, and possessed of a strong
personality matched by few local bishops.

Apostolic Delegate

Archbishop Prigione is central to both the Vatican's influence
and to advances made by the Mexican church in recent years.
Born in 1921 in Castellazzo Bormida, Italy, he majored in
canon law at the Pontifical Lateran University in Rome. After
earning a doctorate in philosophy and letters from the State
University of Rome, he studied at the Vatican's School of
Diplomacy. Prigione held diplomatic posts in Italy, Great
Britain, the United States, Austria, and the International

Table 2
Vatican Representatives to Mexico, 1851–1992

Name	Titular Diocese	Status	Arrival	Departure
Luigi Clementi	Damascus	AD[a]	1851	1861
Pietro Francesco Megalia	Damascus	AN	Dec. 1864	June 1865
Nicola Averardi	Tarsus	AV	1896	1899
Ricardo Sanz di Samper		EE	1902	(Feb./July)
Domenico Serafini, O.S.B.	Spoleto	AD	1904	1905
Giuseppe Ridolfi	Todi-Apamea	AD	1905	1911
Tomasso Boggiania	Edesa	AD	1912	1914
Giovanni Bonzano	Melitene	CA	1915	1921
Ernesto Filippi	Sardica	AD	1921	1923
Serafino Cimino, O.F.M.	Cirro	AD	1925	(Apr./May)
Giorgio Giuseppe Caruana	Sebastea	AD	1926	(Mar./May)
Leopoldo Ruiz y Flores	Morelia	AD	1929	1937
Luis María Martínez	Mexico	CA	1937	1948
Guillermo Piani, S.D.B.[b]	Nicosia	AV/AD	1948	1956
Luigi Raimondi	Tarsus	AD	1956	1967
Guido del Mectri	Tuscania	AD	1967	1970
Carlo Martini	Abari	AD	1970	1973
Mario Pio Gaspair	Numidia	AD	1973	1977
Sotero Sanz Villaba[c]	Merida Augusta	AD	1977	
Jerónimo Prigione	Lauriaco	AD	1978	

Source: Francisco Ramírez M., "Representantes de la santa sede en el mundo y en méxico de 1851 a 1990," in José Trinidad González R., ed., Relaciones iglesia-estado en méxico (Mexico City: Librería Parroquial de Clavería, 1990), 20.

[a]These abbreviations signify apostolic delegate (AD), apostolic nuncio (AN), apostolic visitor (AV), extraordinary envoy (EE), and chargé d'affaires (CA).

[b]Piani served as apostolic visitor before becoming apostolic delegate in 1951.

[c]Died before reaching Mexico.

Atomic Energy Agency before being named apostolic nuncio to El Salvador and Guatemala (1969 to 1974). It was in this assignment that he began to learn about Mexico.

Following four years in Africa, he was sent to Mexico as apostolic delegate in February 1978. The 14 years that he had spent in Mexico by mid-1992 meant that his tenure was nearly three times longer than the average (five years) for his 18 predecessors, a number of whom failed either to master Spanish or interest themselves in the affairs of the Mexican church as Prigione has done. (See table 2.)

As apostolic delegate, Prigione has served as an extremely active liaison between the Holy See and Mexico's episcopate. Among other functions, he makes recommendations on new bishops to be named by the Vatican. More than one-third of the country's 93 active bishops have been appointed with his imprimatur.[21]

Indeed, he views his most important role as "choosing good bishops—men of the church who are not politicians . . . [for] bishops should be a unifying factor in their diocese, not a source of friction and discord." With respect to the selection process, he emphasized that he had recommended "no conservatives and no radicals," but priests who were moderates.[22] Furthermore, he has recommended the creation of coadjutor bishops. These men are supposedly assistants to the ordinary, yet they may eclipse the bishop in influence, especially if they boast close ties to the apostolic delegate.

A case in point is that of Oaxaca. Amid allegations in the late 1980s that the local archbishop, Bartolomé Carrasco Briseño, was unable to enforce celibacy among the 180 priests in this impoverished southwestern state, Prigione recommended that Héctor González Martínez be named Carrasco's coadjutor. Once the change was made, in April 1988, the Vatican invested Carrasco with responsibility for apostolic functions. Meanwhile, Rome placed González Martínez in charge of the local clergy, which ensured his effective control of the archdiocese. The tolerant, amiable Carrasco had encouraged his socially active priests, may of whom did live with women, to work among the poverty-stricken Indians of the region to better their condition and raise their consciousness.

To combat what he perceived as "radicalism and polarization," González Martínez stressed prayer, spiritualism, and individual piety. In addition, he removed teachers and restructured the curriculum of the local seminary to curb the dissemination of liberationist views. Progressive priests in the state protested this change. Prigione told them that, although he hoped the situation would never arise, in a conflict between the 71-year-old Carrasco and González Martínez, the "last word belongs to the coadjutor."[23] Similarly, deaths and retirements of activist bishops in Ciudad Juárez, Tapachula, and Chihuahua have weakened the influence of liberation theology.

Soon after the election of de la Madrid in 1982, the outgoing, strong-minded Prigione began promoting a series of meetings, similar to those convened during the presidency of Luis Echeverría Alvarez. These sessions, held at the tree-shaded Apostolic Delegation in the Guadalupe Inn neighborhood, brought senior bishops together with high administrative officials, the most important of whom was Manuel Bartlett Díaz, who had received a Catholic education at the hands of the Marists. Díaz at that time held the post of government secretary, which was the most influential position in the cabinet and analogous to the minister of the interior in West European governments. Prigione, an inveterate tennis player who prides himself on "finding good partners," often invited his guests to play tennis.

Cold and awkward at first, these sessions evolved into a useful dialogue between traditional antagonists. As Prigione expressed it: "I simply wanted to bring together people who rejected one another by hearsay; it was important to have them meet face to face." At the outset, Bartlett stressed the clear-cut dividing line between church and state; later, Prigione recalled the cabinet secretary's saying "as two militants we will find a way out . . . we will get along well."[24] Although he called himself "vaguely" religious, de la Madrid grew up in a pious Catholic family, was baptized, received First Communion, and married in the church.[25] The de la Madrid family held a mass in the Los Pinos presidential palace every Christmas Eve during his administration. The devoutness of de la Madrid's wife, Paloma, contributed to the good rapport that the president enjoyed with Prigione.

De la Madrid's hand-picked successor, Salinas, has even more assiduously cultivated the 71-year-old Vatican diplomat. Although baptized, confirmed, and married in the church, Salinas is not a practicing Catholic (his wife is a Catholic and masses are occasionally held in Los Pinos). Nevertheless, he gave Prigione a red phone that connected the president's office with the Apostolic Delegation—a symbol of the open lines of communication that both men wish to maintain.

The Apostolic Delegation is a beehive of activity. Prigione regularly welcomes churchmen, diplomats, scholars, business-men, legislators, and cabinet and subcabinet officials to his residence for tennis and the exchange of ideas. Besides PRI leaders, members of the PAN, the Democratic Revolutionary Party (PRD), the conservative Authentic Party of the Mexican Revolution (PARM), and the conservative Catholic Mexican Democratic Party (PDM) have visited Prigione's residence.[26]

Critics complain that the apostolic delegate is a "procon-sul." And Prigione himself said that he has been called a "second Negroponte"—a reference to U. S. ambassador John Negroponte, known for his intensity, intelligence, high energy level, and assiduous quest for contacts. Still, one foreign diplomat, who asked to remain anonymous, said that "Prigione breaks all the rules in intervening in domestic Mexican affairs. If Negroponte were half as intrusive as Prigione he would be PNG'd [declared persona non grata] in a heartbeat." Prigione responds that, unlike other envoys, he defends Mexicans, not foreigners, vis-à-vis their own government.[27] Some critics have labeled the archbishop "PRIgione," suggesting that the first three letters in his name symbolize his fondness for leaders of the revolutionary party.

Prigione realizes that his activist style could breed resent-ment, particularly among the far less dynamic Mexican bishops. To blunt charges that he is a Machiavellian loner, the apostolic delegate usually invites CEM leaders—for example, the presi-dent, vice president, and secretary general—to accompany him to meetings with government officials.[28] Prigione underlines his quest for CEM harmony, but he admits that when a bishop—Méndez Arceo or Ruiz, for example—"sings out of tune with the chorus," he does not hesitate to criticize such behavior.[29]

Prigione and Cardinal Corripio have differed on one issue: the establishment of a separate diocese for the Basilica of Guadalupe. The apostolic delegate joins the highly popular, politically well-connected abbot of the basilica, Guillermo Schulenburg Prado, in supporting such a change. He argues that the shrine requires its own seminary and clergy to meet the special needs of the more than 10 million people who visit the religious center each year. After all, he points out, the most important Marian shrines—Lourdes (France), Fatima (Portugal), and Aparecida (Brazil)—have their own dioceses.[30] Thus far, Corripio has prevailed with his position that the basilica, the jewel in the crown of his realm, should remain within the Archdiocese of Mexico City.

Prigione assumed a new function in May 1990. The Juárez government had severed diplomatic relations with the Vatican in 1857. In February 1990 Salinas named Agustín Téllez Cruces, a distinguished public figure, as his "personal envoy" to the Vatican, an action discussed in chapter 4. As a quid pro quo, Pope John Paul II appointed the apostolic delegate as his "special permanent envoy." As such, Prigione received both a diplomatic passport and license tags.[31] Later, the government provided around-the-clock police protection when five members of the Party of the Poor staged a sit-in the Apostolic Delegation on October 31, 1990.

Churchmen and Politicians

High churchmen offer a fascinating contrast to their political counterparts. As reflected in table 3, in 1990 active bishops (average age 62.5 years) were older than governors (52.1) and were much less likely to be presiding in or near their place of birth. In addition, the prelates held more university degrees, but evinced less experience in Mexico City, which is the Mexican equivalent of "inside the Beltway."

Mexican scholar Roderic Ai Camp has reported unusually interesting recruitment patterns among political and church elites. Bishops, like politicians, select their disciples early in their careers. These men may be singled out for advanced training. As opposed to politicians who, if they attend a university abroad, usually do so in the United States, Mexican clergy-

Table 3
Bishops and Governors, 1990

	Average Age	Number Born in State of Current Service	% Total	Number Born in State Contiguous to State of Current Service	% Total
Bishops (93)	62.5	22	23.7	19	20.4
Governors (30)	52.1	28	93.3	1	3.3

Source: Conferencia del Episcopado Mexicano, *Directorio 1989/1991* (Mexico City: CEM, 1990), 113-124. For biographical data on 30 of Mexico's 31 governors, I am indebted to Miguel Medina H., Documentation Center, PRI, Mexico City.

men are more likely to have studied in Europe—at the Pio Nono Latin American College of the Gregorian University or, since the mid-1970s, at the Gregorian's Mexican College in Rome.

Moreover, politicians come from middle- and upper-middle-class origins, while priests exhibit middle-class backgrounds. As in the Mexican military, "staff clergy" are those who enjoy the greatest mobility. These are priests who spend little or no time in parishes. Instead, they devote themselves to teaching in seminaries, performing administrative duties, and serving as diocesan staff members or as aides to bishops.[32]

Also, politicians boast generational, kinship, educational, and professional links with other government officials, entrepreneurs, and intellectuals—often through networks known as *camarillas.* In contrast, the total number of clergy is small, there are few bishops, and they do not marry to produce children to compose the political families that are so prevalent in Mexico.

Doubtless, clergymen have ample contacts with the National Action Party because its adherents (or *panistas*) frequently attend and teach at parochial schools, particularly in northern states and Mexico City.[33] In addition, political office-

Table 4
Ratio of Priests to Population in Latin America, 1989

Country	Total Population	Roman Catholic Population	Roman Catholic Population as % of Total Population	Number of Priests	Number of Roman Catholics per Priest
Brazil	147,400,000	129,554,000	88.0	13,922	9,305
Mexico	84,270,000	80,541,000	95.6	11,317	7,116
Argentina	31,930,000	29,044,000	91.0	5,605	5,180
Colombia	31,190,000	29,267,000	93.8	6,010	4,870
Peru	21,790,000	20,043,000	92.0	2,438	8,221
Venezuela	19,250,000	17,636,000	91.6	2,044	8,628
Chile	12,960,000	10,512,000	81.1	2,690	3,907
Cuba	10,520,000	4,337,000	41.2	224	19,362
Ecuador	10,490,000	9,747,000	93.0	1,582	6,161
Guatemala	8,930,000	7,442,000	83.3	674	11,041
Bolivia	7,190,000	6,650,000	92.5	925	7,189
Dominican Rep.	7,020,000	6,375,000	90.8	559	11,404
Haiti	5,610,000	5,022,000	89.5	480	10,795
El Salvador	5,210,000	4,782,000	91.8	443	16,967
Honduras	4,950,000	4,632,000	93.4	273	6,785
Paraguay	4,160,000	3,847,000	92.4	576	3,297
Uruguay	3,080,000	2,387,000	77.5	724	3,297
Nicaragua	3,740,000	3,393,000	90.7	315	10,771
Costa Rica	2,920,000	2,584,000	88.5	572	4,517
Panama	2,370,000	2,085,000	87.9	332	6,280
Total	**424,980,000**	**379,880,000**	**89.4**	**51,696**	**7,348**

Source: Felician A. Foy, ed., 1992 Catholic Almanac (Huntington, Ind.: Our Sunday Visitor, Inc. 1991).

holders serve in posts for a fixed number of years. Failure to please a superior or to back a rising political star may abbreviate a career. Catholic leadership is considerably more stable inasmuch as bishops serve long periods, usually until retirement age.[34]

As revealed in table 4, in 1989 the number of Mexican Catholics per priest (7,116) was below the average for Latin America (7,348). In 1945, there had been only 5,380 Mexican Catholics per priest. The number rose because although the country boasted 268 percent more priests in 1989 (11,317) than in 1945 (4,220), the population shot up nearly fourfold during this 44-year period, and the number of vocations did not keep pace with the population growth. This may change because church leaders report that, in contrast to a few years ago when most seminarians were quite young, an ever larger percentage of prospective priests are older, mature men, who have left a profession to enter the clergy.[35]

The shortage of priests aside, Mexico registered one of the highest rates of baptisms in Latin America between 1972 and 1989, the last year for which figures are available. Still, the number of baptisms per 1,000 Catholics has decreased from 37 to 28.2. A successful family planning campaign launched in the early 1970s led to a decline in the birthrate, which helps to explain the fall in baptisms as noted in table 5.

Another reason may be the headway made by Protestant denominations and evangelical sects, which increased their numbers 183 percent between 1980 and 1985, according to Catholic bishops.[36] Included under this rubric are Baptists, Methodists, Jehovah's Witnesses, Mormons, Seventh Day Adventists, Pentecostals, Nazarenes, and dozens of other faiths that are particularly active along the country's southern border and, to a lesser extent, its northern frontier. Limited ecumenical contacts take place between the mainstream Protestant denominations and Roman Catholic authorities. In contrast, the evangelicals openly denigrate Catholicism and seek, under the rubric of the Evangelization 2000 program, to convert half of Latin America's population to their faith by the beginning of the next century.

Table 5
Catholic Baptisms per 1,000 Catholics,
Selected Years, 1972–1989

	1972	1975	1980[a]	1982	1985	1989
Argentina	21.7	21.7	24.8	23.4	21.5	21.44
Bolivia	25.7	25.5	31.0	32.6	31.4	30.31
Brazil	27.8	26.1	25.1	24.9	22.2	20.10
Chile	17.9	18.0	19.4	19.2	17.5	19.32
Colombia	32.1	18.0	27.7	26.7	27.4	26.01
Costa Rica	31.6	27.9	25.8	28.9	31.2	30.07
Cuba	16.5	10.2	4.9	5.3	6.4	19.51
Dominican Republic	21.1	18.9	18.3	16.3	18.2	11.27
Ecuador	30.2	32.8	27.3	25.8	24.8	23.38
El Salvador	30.0	28.8	17.9	23.5	21.4	21.01
Guatemala	30.9	35.9	29.6	29.9	30.5	34.43
Haiti	23.7	21.8	21.0	21.0	21.4	22.76
Honduras	32.4	27.5	30.7	26.5	18.1	15.96
Mexico	37.0	35.6	30.4	27.7	28.1	28.23
Nicaragua	31.6	31.8	27.5	25.0	28.4	25.55
Panama	26.3	25.3	20.7	20.4	18.5	16.96
Paraguay	27.2	28.6	32.1	30.3	29.1	30.74
Peru	26.9	23.5	25.8	26.5	25.1	20.67
Uruguay	15.2	14.6	18.3	17.7	18.2	17.87
Venezuela	27.1	25.8	27.2	26.5	22.2	23.87

Source: James W. Wilkie, ed., *Statistical Abstract of Latin America,* vol. 27 (Los Angeles: UCLA Latin American Center Publications, 1989), 259; Data for 1972 and 1975 from Consejo Episcopal Latinoamericano (CELAM), *Iglesia y américa latina cifras, 1978,* 6: 1980 data adapted from Felician A. Foy, ed., *1990 Catholic Almanac* (Huntington, Ind.: Our Sunday Visitor, Inc., 1989) and *1992 Catholic Almanac* (Huntington, Ind.: Our Sunday Visitor, Inc., 1991).

[a]Data for 1980–1989 represent figures as of December 31 for each corresponding year.

Lay Organizations

Even though the topic is beyond the scope of this monograph, it should be noted that various lay organizations cooperate closely with Mexico's Roman Catholic clergy. As suggested in chapter 1, most important among these groups is the National Action Party. Despite the PAN's pro-Catholic orientation, the church has avoided endorsing or identifying with it or any other political party lest it compromise its moral position, attenuate its evangelizing mission, and alienate the PRI. In 1990 the PAN nominated two ex-priests to run for the Zacatecas state legislature. Neither claimed the church's endorsement. Indeed, PAN standard-bearer Vicente Fox, an attractive businessman who lost the August 18, 1991, gubernatorial election in Guanajuato amid charges of ubiquitous PRI-inspired fraud, averred that the church hierarchy had provided little assistance to PAN candidates compared with past years.[37]

In 1922 Pope Pius XI authorized the foundation of lay Catholic Action groups throughout the church designed to penetrate key layers of society deemed to have been neglected by the church. In his view, the movement would promote "cooperation of all Catholic people, men and women, boys and girls, in the apostleship of the Catholic hierarchy."[38] In 1951 Archbishop Martínez mobilized these groups in a national campaign for morality that he himself headed.

A study published in the 1950s reported the following memberships for the four Catholic Action branches: Union of Catholic Men, whose members are married men or those 35 years of age or older, 44,000; Catholic Women's Union, composed of 198,052 teachers, urban workers, and campesinas; Male Youth, embracing 18,000 adherents between ages 15 and 35; and Female Youth, made up of 88,221 members between ages 15 and 35. The archbishop's mobilizing effort reached its climax in 1953 with "the largest national assembly of Catholic leaders since the beginning of the revolution."[39]

Other lay groups include the National Parents' Union (500,000 members), the Knights of Columbus (3,500), the Mexican Legion of Decency (800), the National Association of Journalists, Writers, Publicists, and Editors (425), and the National Work of the Good Press (Obra Nacional de la Buena

Prensa). Between 1936 and 1952, the latter organization published millions of copies of books, magazines, and pamphlets.[40]

Church-related organizations also play a large role in education, which is surprising in view of Article 3's unambiguous language about lay instruction. As reflected in table 6, 7.24 percent of the nation's almost 25.5 million students attend 1,165 Catholic primary, secondary, or advanced-level schools. It is estimated that approximately 323,000 million pesos (U.S. $120 million) are expended monthly in tuition payments. With respect to social origins, 14 percent of the Catholic school population is lower class, 47 percent lower middle class, and 21 percent upper class.[41]

Ten thousand religious operate these schools—with sisters in charge of six times as many schools (994) as brothers (171). Las Hermanas de los Pobres Siervas del Sagrado Corazón, Las Hermanas Josefinas de México, and Las Hermanas de las Escuelas Cristianas are the most prominent congregations in education.

Catholic schools are situated throughout the nation, but they are disproportionately concentrated in the Federal District and the states of Michoacán, Guanajuato, Jalisco, San Luis Potosí, and México. Father Andrés Delgado Hernández, executive secretary of the Episcopal Commission for Education and Culture, reported that there are two applicants for every place in a parochial school.[42] The 13 Catholic universities are also attractive to students.

Opus Dei is a discreet organization devoted to "Christianizing" society as a lay institute. Once renowned for secrecy, Opus Dei has enjoyed Pope John Paul II's quiet encouragement and is assuming a slightly higher profile—with increasing attention devoted to recruitment in Mexico and other Third World countries. Although the Catholic church is having difficulty attracting new clerical vocations in the United States and Western Europe, Opus Dei has grown worldwide until it now boasts some 75,000 members in 47 countries. Thus, it is three times larger than the Society of Jesus, the largest religious order.

Opus Dei is run by priests, but lay people compose more than 98 percent of its membership, which is made up of ap-

Table 6
Student Enrollment in Public, Catholic, and Other Private Schools, 1988–1989

Educational Level	Public[a]	%	Catholic	%	Other Private	%	Subtotal	%	%[b]
Preschool	2,495,900	92.42	153,375	5.67	51,125	1.85	2,700,400	100	10.99
Primary	13,785,000	95.35	600,000	4.51	165,000	1.12	14,610,000	100	57.31
Vocational	144,520	32.22	273,600	61.00	30,400	6.77	448,520	100	1.75
Secondary School	4,026,800	91.68	203,016	5.98	102,284	2.32	4,392,100	100	17.23
Trade School	297,370	65.01	88,000	19.24	72,000	15.74	457,370	100	1.79
High School (Middle School & Preparatory)	1,261,000	77.07	255,000	15.58	120,000	7.33	1,636,000	100	6.42
Teacher Training	92,700	67.86	30,730	22.49	13,170	9.64	136,600	100	0.53
University	950,000	85.58	121,600	10.95	38,400	3.45	1,110,040	100	4.35
Total	23,053,290	90.43	1,845,321	7.24	592,379	2.32	25,490,990	100	100

Source: Excélsior, April 24, 1990, p. 43-A; Estimates provided by the secretary of public education, National Bank of Mexico, and the National Confederation of Private Schools.

[a]Includes state and federal educational institutions.

[b]Nationwide percentage enrolled at each level.

proximately equal numbers of men and women. Members are divided into "numeraries," who accept vows of chastity and live in communities; "associates," who are also celibate but live independently; and "supernumeraries," who can live at home, marry, and raise children. The great majority hold secular jobs, many in key financial, business, and academic centers. They are expected to give a substantial portion of their income to the movement.[43]

Founded in 1949, Mexico's branch of Opus Dei has roughly 5,000 members.[44] Many of these men and women are especially well placed in business, although some hold government posts. The Pan American Executive Institute (IPADE) is the cradle of Opus Dei activity in the country. IPADE is the moving force behind the church-run Pan American University in Mexico City. Reportedly, other institutions influenced by Opus Dei are Escuela Cedros, Escuela Mexicana de Turismo, and the Residencia Universitaria Panamericana.[45]

Thanks to Vatican backing and the esprit de corps of its elite membership, Opus Dei thrives even as lay groups in general have declined in influence, particularly those associated with Catholic Action. Organizations such as the National Parents' Union and the Pro-Life Committee report a large number of adherents; nonetheless, they seem to have more members on paper than they can activate for political purposes.[46] During his visit to Mexico in May 1990, the pope chided Mexican Catholics for their inactivity. "By no means can faithful laymen abdicate participation in politics—that is, in manifold and diverse cultural, administrative, legislative, social, and economic action designed to promote . . . the common good."[47]

Over the years, various extreme right-wing groups have emerged flying the Catholic banner and espousing virulent anti-Communist and neo-Fascist views. Most notable was the National Sinarchist Union (UNS), which was discussed in chapter 1. World War II left the *sinarquistas* discredited and divided—with the movement's strength concentrated in Guanajuato. After a political reform in 1978, the UNS evolved into the Mexican Democratic Party, which lost its official registration in 1988 when its presidential nominee captured only 1.04 percent of the votes cast.

Jalisco provides the home base for the right-wing TECOS, who were also organized in the 1930s in the town of Tecomán, which may be the source of the organization's name. This group appeared about the same time that the Autonomous University of Guadalajara was founded to preserve Western, Christian values in the face of Cárdenas's "socialist" reforms. As an elite, vanguard organization, the TECOS recruit among the university's students who display intellectual ability and leadership skills.

Like an onion, the TECOS exhibit many layers. The casual observer notes the movement's conspicuous role in the university's cultural, social, and athletic life. At its core, however, it is an intransigently anti-Communist group, many of whose members have excelled in the business world and professions while keeping a sharp eye on state and national politics.[48]

TECOS, who work openly and profess obedience to the church, appear moderate compared to the University Movement of Renovating Direction (MURO). Students in the Department of Economics at the National Autonomous University of Mexico (UNAM) formed this shadowy, ultraconservative organization in 1961 in reaction to Castro's ascent to power. Its aggressive anticommunism and eagerness to disrupt liberal and leftist meetings earned MURO the reputation of being a "fascist university clique."[49] This penchant for violence combined with a virulent hostility toward progressive priests prompted the archbishop of Mexico City to prohibit students in Catholic schools from affiliating with the organization.[50]

Why have most traditional lay organizations declined in importance? First, like the formal church structure itself, they lack leadership and have not attracted someone like Archbishop Prigione to activate them. Second, in contrast to the harsh repression suffered by Catholics in the 1920s, the government has long since replaced persecution of the faithful with a live-and-let-live policy. Such conciliation diminishes the need for organized efforts to protect the church from repression. Third, although the PRI-dominated regime no longer shoots or incarcerates religious militants, it can still punish perceived troublemakers by withholding government contracts, jobs, and political posts. The administration's ability to use economic pressures greatly expanded between 1970 and 1982 as the public sector grew by leaps and bounds. Fourth, anticommunism, the cause that successfully mobilized lay people in the 1950s, has declined as a rallying cry because of the disintegration of the Soviet Union. Fifth, during the past generation, the government has sedulously avoided stirring up Catholics by impeding efforts to legalize abortion in Chiapas and Quintana Roo.[51] This is a "hot button" issue for many members of the hierarchy, as well as for both the National Parents' Union and the Pro-Life Committee. Finally, in encouraging more openness and greater lay participation in the ministry of the church, Vatican II may have diverted Catholic activists away from traditional organizations to involvement in parishes and base communities.

3
From Quiescence to Activism (1958–1988)

As part of the post-*Cristero* rebellion accord, the Roman Catholic hierarchy largely curtailed the social activism that had placed it at odds with the state. Meanwhile, the church promoted various programs to encourage peaceful change. It spawned some 500 *cajas populares* or savings and loan institutions that, by 1967, had 29,000 members and had registered loans totaling almost 24 million pesos. In Guanajuato, the church's Center of Agrarian Social Development trained farmers who could impart their skills, like rural extension agents in the United States, to other members of their community. The Jesuit-run Industrial Technical School of Torreón emulated the Guanajuato project—with the goal of inculcating industrial skills in prospective union leaders infused with Christian values. The National Guadalupean Association of Mexican Workers also shared this dual purpose of training union leaders and promoting religious instruction amid a period of declining religious commitment.[1]

End to Quietism

Several events occurred in the 1960s and 1970s that brought an end to the church's social quietism. The first was the institution by President Adolfo López Mateos (1958–1964) of a system of free and compulsory textbooks, the *texto único*. The episcopate decried this 1960 initiative as "totalitarian" because, it alleged, the books negatively portrayed the church as an obstacle to national development. Yet, consistent with the informal rules of the game hammered out a generation before, the bishops remained at the margin of the battle, sending proxies into the fray—notably the PAN and the National Parents' Union. Secret negotiations at the highest levels of state and church prevented a crisis. The secretary of education agreed to remove some offending passages. For instance, one volume presented pictures of a young boy and girl, scantily clad, on opposite pages; when the book was closed, they came together suggestively—an invitation for students to titillate each other. Placing the pictures back-to-back restored decorum and defused parental complaints.[2]

Even more important in stirring the church was the Latin American Episcopal Conference, which since its organization in 1955 had become a major instrument for disseminating the social gospel. Composed of all Latin American prelates, it promoted modernization and spread reforms emanating not only from the Holy See but also from progressive churchmen throughout Western Europe. Pope Paul VI attended the second CELAM conclave held in Medellín, Colombia, in 1968. Here, he related to Latin America the themes that had been raised at the Second Vatican Council and embellished in the encyclicals *Mater et Magistra, Pacem in Terris,* and *Populorum Progressio.*

Specifically, he urged that the church, long associated with the established order, should fulfill its sacred mission by discarding its cautious, otherworldly orientation and actively casting its lot with the poor, the humble, the downtrodden, and the powerless. The pontiff vigorously decried injustice and oppression and, with equal fervor, championed peaceful social change. Violence, he insisted, was both unchristian and antievangelical. The bishops contemplated his words before crafting a new definition of violence that embraced not simply physical aggression but also coercive acts inherent in the unjust and exploitative societies that pervaded Latin America. Overcoming such "institutionalized violence" might require, as a last resort, violent acts against the "sinful social system" to replace it with a more just order. "In this light, political action can be legitimated in terms of liberation from sin, itself clearly a central mission of the church."[3]

With respect to the poor, the Medellín conference adopted a sociological definition. No longer was poverty viewed as a product of personal shortcomings or misfortune to be alleviated by charity alone; rather, it derived from unjust social structures whose dismantling required political initiatives. In its pursuit of equality and justice, the church—inspired by the example of Old Testament prophets—should make common cause with the poor.[4] Needless to say, Medellín-motivated challenges to traditional elites raised hackles in jockey clubs, executive suites, and presidential palaces throughout the region.

The final Medellín document highlighted the two massive evils plaguing the region: external domination and internal colonialism. The church would have to precipitate change to prevent being overcome by it. Thus, it was necessary to reach out to the oppressed of the continent through evangelization and lay participation focused on base communities.

Such a philosophy directly confronted the church's experience in Mexico, where for most of five centuries a majority of its hierarchy had cooperated with, or acquiesced in, rule by the affluent and the powerful. Many bishops still dragged their feet, but the concept of change in behalf of the poor now enjoyed unimpeachable legitimacy.[5]

Animated by the spirit of Medellín, such progressive groups as Christians for Socialism (Cristianos para el Socialismo) and Priests for the People (Sacerdotes para el Pueblo) sprang to life in Mexico. These organizations gave impetus to the base community movement that flourished in the late 1960s and early 1970s.

Even as social effervescence grew at the grass-roots level, the government's fierce repression of the student activists in 1968 encouraged the church hierarchy to adopt a prudent relationship with the civil powers. During the 20-year-plus "economic miracle" that followed World War II, the political system had furnished opportunities for members of the growing and increasingly heterogeneous middle class. True, they looked askance at the authoritarianism, corruption, and curbs on free expression that blemished the regime; yet the system generated both jobs for themselves and social mobility for their children. Flagging growth, however, exacerbated political tensions.

In 1968 student dissatisfaction with political conditions and economic inequality sparked at least 47 separate demonstrations between July 23 and August 10. In mid-August, the student strike committee shifted from a series of minor protests to a mass rally that drew 150,000 demonstrators to the Zócalo in central Mexico City on August 13. There the protesters decried the link between President Gustavo Díaz Ordaz and police and army violence in placards that scorned the chief executive as: "Criminal," "Hated Beast," and "Assassin."[6]

The impending Olympic Games sharpened government concerns about the mounting protests. These contests were to be held in Mexico City and, it was hoped, would project to the world the image of a modern, enterprising, and peaceable country. The climax of the government-student conflict took place on October 2, 1968, in the Tlatelolco area of Mexico City, however, when army and police units killed hundreds of unarmed students, housewives, and office workers who were protesting the lack of freedom in their country. Three years later, a similar, though somewhat less bloody, crackdown took place in Mexico City.

Luis Echeverría Alvarez was president during this second incident. An atheist who had been government secretary at the time of the "Tlatelolco massacre," he had shown no sympathy for the church during 25 years in public life. Nevertheless, he collaborated closely with the hierarchy.

A possible explanation for his behavior may have been the chief executive's quest for allies. His penchant for greater state control of the economy offended many members of the business community. Thus, the self-proclaimed "people's president" increasingly courted peasants and workers. Apparently, this populist strategy included appeals to Roman Catholics, and the presidential gambit coincided with efforts to activate the Mexican church. In 1971 the synod of Catholic bishops held in Rome published a report entitled "Justice in Mexico." This document criticized the dearth of social and economic justice in the country and blamed the condition, in part, on the lack of church leadership. Thereafter, the CEM gave social issues a notably higher priority.

In 1972 Echeverría executed a volte-face on population matters. Once a pronatalist, he became an advocate of family planning as social problems mounted with the birthrate. This policy shift could have produced a clash with the episcopate. To obviate friction in this period, government authorities regularly conferred with church representatives.[7] Population issues more than likely figured in these discussions. In any

case, the 1973 General Population Law diplomatically emphasized "responsible parenthood." This theme, which had appeared in the 1968 encyclical *Humanae Vitae*, conveyed the
idea that voluntary family planning, not intrusive official
action, would characterize Mexico's demographic policy.[8]

In keeping with his good will toward the church,
Echeverría sought Pope Paul VI's endorsement of his "Charter
of Economic Rights and Duties of States." This proposal, which
formed part of an attempt to create a "New International
Economic Order," emphasized the North-South division
between affluent, industrialized states (concentrated in the
Northern Hemisphere) and impecunious, developing nations
(clustered in the Southern Hemisphere). The charter proposed
to assist the latter by restructuring world economic relations.
Recommendations included controls on exploitative multinational corporations, trade concessions for primary product
exporters, and expanded flows of development capital from the
First to the Third World.[9]

In mid-1973, the pontiff sent a message expressing his
appreciation and approval of the Mexican chief executive's
initiative. Echeverría took advantage of this overture to obtain
a papal audience on February 9, 1974, thus becoming the first
incumbent Mexican president to visit the Vatican. The pontiff
gave his visitor a highly symbolic gift: a bronze relief of St.
Paul falling from his horse on the road to Damascus, the
incident in which the erstwhile persecutor of Christians was
converted to the faith.[10] A spokesman for the Mexican church
expressed cynicism about Paul VI's reception of Echeverría:
"The pope even blesses animals," he told me with a mischie-
vous smile.[11]

Church-state collaboration was also evident in the late
1974 announcement by ecclesiastical authorities that a new
Basilica of Guadalupe would be constructed. Crucial to this
undertaking was generous government assistance, particularly
in obtaining corporate contributions.[12] Echeverría, who often
visited the home of Abbot Schulenburg, treated the project as
a major accomplishment of his administration. The shrine's
opening just two months before the chief executive left office
further underscored the political motives associated with its

construction. Doubtless, the ambitious president, so soon to be out of office, desired the church's assistance in his pursuit of two goals: the Nobel Peace Prize and the United Nations (UN) secretary generalship.

Paul VI had no interest in assisting Echeverría's efforts. Then in ill health, the pontiff politely refused an invitation to inaugurate the basilica. The Holy Father's message, transmitted on the day of the festivities, indirectly raised a concern of many progressive Catholics—namely, the gap between the enormous wealth lavished on the shrine and the shameful poverty suffered by so many of the Virgin's devotees.[13]

Throughout the 1970s, the church also strengthened its ties to key politicians—with Abbot Schulenburg often serving as a channel of communications between Roman Catholic leaders and the government. In addition, the church improved its access to the mass media, broadened its role in education, honed its ability to mobilize the faithful, and sought to resolve intraecclesiastical conflicts.[14] With respect to the last point, the 1977 selection of Corripio to succeed Dario Miranda y Gómez as Mexico City's cardinal appeared to be a compromise between traditional and progressive elements of the hierarchy.

Echeverría's successor, José López Portillo, broadened opportunities for involvement by groups outside the PRI's political family. During his electoral campaign, López Portillo met privately with more than 40 bishops. Once in office, he endorsed the Law of Political Organizations and Electoral Processes (LOPPE). This reform encouraged the creation of new parties, ensured their access to radio and television, and expanded the opposition's presence in an enlarged Chamber of Deputies.[15] Although it was not directly relevant to the church, the LOPPE epitomized the greater tolerance permitted by Mexico's elites. By increasing avenues of access to policy-making, the framers of the new statute hoped to keep political adversaries in the system, thereby dissuading extremists from trading ballots for bullets.

Pope John Paul II

Pope John Paul II's visit to Mexico in January 1979, his first international trip after his elevation to the papacy, gave evidence of the church's "convocatory power." This phenomenon connotes the ability to establish rapport with the masses—a skill enhanced by Karol Jozef Wojtyla's background as a professor and actor.[16] At a time when the government had to truck in and feed people to fill a city plaza for a presidential speech, the largest crowds in Mexican history flocked to see the pope. Many onlookers spontaneously burst into tears, frantically crossed themselves, kissed the shadow cast by the pontiff as his motorcade rumbled by, waved white and yellow Vatican flags, or cheered "Bless us, Father, bless our home." During his five-day visit, an estimated 15 million men, women, and children attended his masses or applauded him as he rode in the "popemobile," a converted pickup truck encased in a transparent security shield designed to allow the multitudes to see him as he passed through the streets of major cities. Those who failed to obtain a first-hand view followed the pontiff's journey through telecasts sponsored by Mexico's largest banks and corporations.

What accounted for the tumultuous welcome? To begin with, Mexicans are an overwhelmingly Catholic people who could be expected to demonstrate enthusiasm for the leader of their faith. Too, Mexico was the first foreign country visited by the Polish pope, the first non-Italian successor to Peter since the ascetic Dutchman, Hadrian VI (1522–1523). In addition to being a moral leader, John Paul II possessed what the media call "star quality."

Moreover, the church's new pontiff had expanded Paul VI's commitment to speak out for poor nations. To illuminate the challenge of global poverty, John Paul II adapted to the twentieth century the biblical parable of the banqueter Dives (First World) and the poor man Lazarus (Third World), who ate table scraps.[17] Above all, he epitomized traits deemed conspicuously absent in Mexican politicians: honesty, integrity, humility, concern for the downtrodden, devotion to Christian values, and a strong aversion to violence. No wonder the crowds surged around the eminent visitor.

Even government officials, for whom praising the church was taboo, could not resist the pope's appeal. A local newspaper cartoon cleverly depicted the paradox. It showed a bureaucrat publicly criticizing the pope's presence, while in private he clutched his rosary and jumped for joy.[18] As a "small reminder of the visit," the church erected a bronze statue, six meters in height, of the pontiff in the atrium joining the old to the new Basilica of Guadalupe. Prigione diplomatically attributed to Cardinal Corripio the idea for this sculptured symbol of the Mexico-pope-church trinity.[19]

John Paul II's purpose in visiting Mexico was to address the Third CELAM Assembly of Latin American bishops, held in Puebla. There he attempted to rein in the social activism exhibited in recent years. He condemned interpretations of liberation theology that endorsed Marxism, violence, and class conflict, stressed the absolute authority of the hierarchy in doctrinal matters, and admonished the clergy to spurn partisan politics. "Don't forget," he said, "that temporal leadership can easily be the source of division, while the priest must be a symbol . . . of unity."[20]

The pope's emphasis on authority did not prevent the bishops from exploring the roots of the poverty, injustice, and human rights violations rampant in Latin America. They criticized the lack of economic integration among nations; condemned exploitation at the hands of multinational corporations; deplored the arms race as "the great crime of our time"; backed land reform to uplift the peasantry; scorned greed, venality, and public and private corruption; and bemoaned the prevalence of material over moral values. Compared to Medellín, "Puebla had a much greater impact in Mexico and not simply because the conference took place within its borders. This time the Mexican bishops were strongly influenced by movements from below and by Mexican intellectual circles."[21]

The papal visit came amid the oil boom that politicians promised would make Mexico "permanently prosperous," thereby overcoming the evils identified at Puebla. The gross domestic product (GDP) expanded approximately 8 percent each year between 1978 and 1982. Mexico's success became the envy of a world floundering in recession. Such glamor, however, diverted attention from the beginnings of "petrolization." This neologism connoted an overheated economy fueled by oil revenues, an overvalued currency, mounting dependence on external credits to import escalating amounts of food, capital, and luxury goods, a stagnant agricultural sector, and—above all—outsized budget deficits spawned by prodigious public spending. Like a heroin addict who sells his blood in the morning to get a "fix" from an eager, well-heeled pusher at night, Mexico coped with the pressures of petrolization by exchanging oil for loans.

The situation changed dramatically after an international oil glut appeared in the spring of 1981. As export earnings plummeted, only a herculean international rescue effort prevented Mexico's economic collapse in mid-1982. The six-year administration of de la Madrid, who took office late that year, witnessed the worst economic crisis to beset Mexico since the Great Depression. Exports sagged, dollar reserves fell, the external debt expanded, unemployment rose, emigration surged, and worker purchasing power declined. The oil-intoxicated Cinderella of the late 1970s had become an ugly stepsister. The church began to speak out on behalf of those who suffered as a result of the economic crisis.

Political Involvement

Especially assertive were Cardinal Corripio and the Mexico City-Puebla-Guadalajara church leadership, the northern prelates, and the southern bishops. Although agreeing on many points, each of these groups had its own priorities.

Corripio and his colleagues were the main practitioners of the so-called Polish strategy (*vía polaca*) advocated by John Paul II. Put briefly, they strove to strengthen the church's position vis-à-vis the state and maintain friendly relations with the government both to win full legal status and advance their religious goals. This mission entailed promoting human dignity, human rights, and social reforms on behalf of the poor. Still, politics loomed large on their agenda. For example, the Mexican bishops published 10 million copies of a pamphlet alerting Catholics to the "danger posed to their faith" by Marxist-Leninist advocates of revolutionary class conflict—a struggle that had produced "so many crimes" in nations in which the Communist Party had seized power. The target of this attack was the United Socialist Party of Mexico (PSUM), which had appealed to Christians for support in the 1982 national elections. The hierarchy denied that the church prohibited Catholics from voting for any particular political party. Nonetheless, it warned Christians that

> to vote for a party inspired by Marxist philosophy is to cooperate in establishing a national situation that presents serious difficulties to the faith; and in this sense represents a vote against the Christian faith. It is impossible to be both a Christian and a Marxist.[22]

Corripio and his cohorts were selective in their attacks on the regime. Adopting an approach similar to the antistatist line of their Polish brethren, they deplored the nationalization of Mexico's banking system in October 1982. In general, their tack was to take advantage of the church's mounting influence, evidenced by the unprecedented crowds attracted by the pope in 1979, to negotiate an improved status for their faith. Above all, they wanted the 1917 Constitution amended to remove the official sword of Damocles that menaced Roman Catholicism.[23]

In mid-1983, the episcopate's secretary general even called for an open debate on whether Article 130 complied with the UN Charter on Human Rights, which Mexico had both signed and championed.[24] Although they were anxious to have the unfettered right to comment on issues of the day, Corripio and his cohorts "would prefer that such activities be limited to members of the hierarchy, with pronouncements by other clerics and religious brothers and sisters subject to the approval of the individual bishops in question."[25] As discussed in chapter 2, relations between CEM leaders and the government improved dramatically during the 1980s, thanks in large part to the interchanges promoted by the apostolic delegate.

Northern Bishops Speak Out

Even as Government Secretary Bartlett held productive parleys with key members of the episcopate, the northern bishops pulled no punches in excoriating official corruption when it affected the PAN most adversely. In 1982 Bishops Talamás Camandari (Ciudad Juárez) and Carlos Quintero Arce (Hermosillo) ridiculed Mexican "democracy" because of the

centralism, venality, demagoguery, immorality, and identification of the regime with an "official party" that characterized
the political system. In May 1983, Quintero Arce took part in a
PAN-sponsored meeting in Sonora. His attendance came on
the heels of a statement by Bishop Reynoso Cervantes (then of
Ciudad Obregón) that the PAN's gubernatorial nominee in
Sonora enjoyed the church's sympathy.[26]

The PAN's candidates in municipal contests throughout
the North also gained in electoral support in 1983. Citizens in
this region, who historically viewed with disdain the central
government in Mexico City, resented de la Madrid's economic
policy. Particularly irksome were the peso devaluations that
greatly reduced purchasing power in the United States, to
which the northern economy is tightly linked. This resent-
ment coincided with the president's pledge to hold fair elections as part of a vaunted "moral renovation" campaign. The
upshot was opposition victories throughout the region. Mayoral
posts fell like tenpins as the PAN scored triumphs in the state
capitals of Chihuahua, Durango, Sonora, and San Luis Potosí.
In Chihuahua alone, the center-right party captured municipal contests in towns containing 75 percent of the state's
population.

Stunned by these resounding setbacks, the PRI flailed out
at the clergy in general, and at Bishop Talamás and Archbishop Adalberto Almeida Merino in particular, for manipulating the voters. Despite these attacks, other Revolutionary
Party candidates sought to identify with the church. In Ciudad
Juárez, the largest city in Chihuahua, supporters of the gov-
ernment-backed mayoral nominee (and his alternate) affixed
to their homes stickers with the following message: "In this
house we are proud to be Catholics and PRI members. On 6
July we will vote for Jaime Bermúdez and Alfredo Ríos."[27]

In any case, the party vowed not to repeat its mistake by
allowing fair counts in elections scheduled for Chihuahua,
Sonora, and Nuevo León in 1985 and 1986. Thus, with journalists and observers from around the world looking on, the PRI
mobilized its political operatives, known as "alchemists," to
transmute electoral defeats into victories. To work their magic,
these modern-day wizards manipulated electoral rolls, voted

the dead, and stuffed ballot boxes. They also disqualified unreliable voters, encouraged multiple voting by flying squads of "aviators," diverted public funds into campaign coffers, finagled the results, and managed local news reports.

The exceptional magnitude of the corruption led northern churchmen to take extraordinary steps. Father Camilo Daniel Pérez, a veteran in the base community movement, helped to create the Democratic Electoral Movement (MED), which launched a civil disobedience campaign. The MED staged rallies, occupied public buildings, blockaded major highways, and staged a sit-down strike on the international bridge linking Ciudad Juárez to El Paso. Bishop Talamás lambasted the government for perverting the people's will and accused those responsible for having sinned against the Lord and their fellow citizens.

These diatribes paled in comparison to Archbishop Almeida's pronouncement of July 13, 1986. Recounting the Good Samaritan parable, he explained that the decent people of Chihuahua had fallen prey to political robbers. To protest this act of banditry, he announced that priests would not hold masses in the archdiocese on July 20. This boycott would constitute "a strong sign on our part to those whose eyes still remain blindfolded or who are blinded by their own guilt."[28]

To suspend the celebration of services evoked the crimson specter of church closings during the *Cristero* rebellion. Alarmed at this prospect, Cardinal Enrique Salazar López of Guadalajara publicly expressed the belief that the archibishop of Chihuahua had gone too far. Meanwhile, Government Secretary Bartlett, taking advantage of the ever more accessible lines of church-state communication, warned Prigione that halting masses would be a provocative act that could engender bloodshed. Prigione, in turn, conveyed this warning to the CEM Presidency, which asked its secretary general to confer with Almeida. The archbishop remained intractable, saying that he could not renege unless the pope intervened. The CEM asked Prigione to contact the Vatican, and Cardinal Achille Silvestrini, a Curia member and key official in the Secretariat of State, told him in no uncertain terms that to suspend masses would violate canon law and that the prelate ordering such action would be disciplined.

Reluctantly, Almeida called off the boycott; he reported, however, that John Paul II condemned the events in Chihuahua. This announcement was, to say the least, a misrepresentation. Even though Rome condemns civil rights abuses in general, neither Silvestrini nor any other papal spokesman had alluded to the electoral situation in Chihuahua.[29] To save face, Almeida ordered the reading, at the July 20 masses, of a strongly worded pastoral against fraud that Chihuahua's bishops had released the previous March. In October they published a pastoral letter entitled "The Road Toward Peace." This missive proposed conciliation with civil authorities but demanded that injustices be corrected, fraud curtailed, and manipulated elections annulled. Clearly, the archbishop of Monterrey was correct in 1985 when he stated that the church would not limit itself "to saying the rosary" as government officials wished, but would strive for a multiparty system for the vigorous expression of political ideas. Wary of mounting clerical activism, the de la Madrid administration encouraged the passage of Article 343 of the New Federal Electoral Code. This measure sharply increased the penalty for priests who involved themselves in politics.

Southern Bishops Back the Poor

Just as their northern counterparts joined elite agitation for electoral reform in their relatively prosperous region, bishops from seven southern Pacific dioceses have lofted the banner of the dispossessed in their impoverished, violence-ridden region, which leads the nation in the number of political prisoners and kidnappings. Their task is made all the more difficult by the ubiquitous fatalism revealed in local places of worship:

> Violence, death, and martyrdom are reflected in the iconography of the Mexican country churches. Wooden figures of Christ are colorful, dripping blood from the Sacred Heart and down from the Crown of Thorns. Central to Mexican Catholicism are the Virgins of Guadalupe and Papoan, symbols of the martyred woman who suffers and gives up her sons to death. It is revealing to listen to a Mexican sermon on the glories of suffering and the rewards of martyrdom. In that the religion centralizes death, it

rationalizes death's omnipresence. Catholicism thus captured and glorified the central theme of successive oppressive societies in Mexico.[30]

Rather than acquiesce in oppression, however, these
southern prelates have steadfastly condemned a land-tenure
system that consigns the majority to filth, malnutrition, and
exploitation. They have denounced the murder of peasants
who run afoul of local landowning barons, many of whom are
PRI stalwarts. In a 1985 pastoral on human rights, Bishop Ruiz
García emphasized the salience of land disputes, documented
the killing of campesinos, reported the eviction of entire
peasant communities, and publicized the burning of Indian
houses.[31] Indeed, local churchmen claim that 102 assassina-
tions and 328 "disappearances" occurred between 1982 and
1988 when a tough-as-nails general, Absalón Castellanos
Domínguez, governed the state as if it were a personal fiefdom.

Repeatedly, Ruiz García and his colleagues have pointed
accusatory fingers at the government for refusing to serve as
"social arbiters" to protect the rights of the dispossessed.
Failure both to implement land reform and to facilitate mar-
keting of traditional crops means that ragged peasants live on
the very edge of subsistence. Malnutrition is their constant
companion, and the prospect of starvation haunts their lives.
Is it any wonder, the bishops argue, that the Indians turn to
the cultivation of marijuana and opium? The prelates have
also charged that government officials work hand in glove with
the drug mafia.[32]

Incensed at this criticism, many local elites accuse the
prelates of being "Mexican Castroites" and "Sandinistas in
clerical garb." Such attacks often connect the churchmen to
gunrunning, assisting Central American rebels, and aiding
such leftist movements as the Isthmian Peasant-Student-
Worker Coalition (COCEI) and the "Plan of Ayala" National
Coordinating Body. Both organizations have attempted to
mobilize peasants whom the PRI egregiously manipulates and
exploits through the National Campesino Confederation, the
largest and weakest of the official party's three sectors. In 1985
some two dozen PRI officials in Tehuantepec announced their
intention to meet with Apostolic Delegate Prigione to seek the

removal of Bishop Lona Reyes from the diocese. Apparently, the meeting never took place.[33]

In 1980 COCEI registered its greatest victory when it won the mayoralty of Juchitán, Oaxaca. An ugly, sometimes bloody, tug-of-war with the PRI over this post lasted until early 1984 when the army evicted the COCEI activists. Although he disclaimed involvement in creating the militant organization, Bishop Lona Reyes pointed to a "coincidence of interests" between the church and COCEI. Both endeavor to raise the peasants' consciousness, to make them aware of how the system exploits them, and to attract allies to the campesinos' cause to obtain social justice.

Even as they have championed the cause of impoverished Mexicans, the bishops have sought to safeguard the refugees who have poured into Chiapas, Mexico's southernmost state, from Guatemala and other Central American countries in recent years. Compounding the danger to the refugees were armed incursions into their camps by hard-core elements of the Guatemalan military. In addition to providing aid, the diocese of San Cristóbal de las Casas continually demanded that the government furnish drinking water, decent food, adequate housing, and health care to the newcomers. Relocating the newcomers to the more distant states of Campeche and Quintana Roo defused an extremely volatile situation. As a result of the dissipation of these tensions in the South, the attention devoted to Bishop Ruiz García, who had publicized the refugees' conditions, declined. Mainstream clerical leaders, who pursued church-state conciliation with Mexico's newly elected president, began to monopolize the spotlight.

*   *   *   *

Often church and state appear on the opposite ends of a legitimacy teeter-totter. The strengthening of the latter in the post-*Cristero* era diminished the influence of the Roman Catholic hierarchy. Conversely, the decline in the state's fortunes after 1968 saw the legitimacy of the church increase.[34] An enormously successful papal visit further boosted the church's stock; it also expanded autonomous activity by the bishops who, thanks to political reforms, could more readily oppose arbitrary state action. The collapse of the oil boom in the 1980s provided a point of convergence for the several factions within the church hierarchy. Each had its own agenda, but all could agree on the need to serve as defenders of social justice and human rights during the worst economic conditions since the Great Depression.[35]

4
Salinas Courts the Church
(1988–1991)

Growing cynicism toward the political system led de la Madrid's successor, Carlos Salinas de Gortari, to make overtures to Mexico's Roman Catholics. In part he wanted to demonstrate his commitment to modernization; in part he hoped to win political support. After all, a dark cloud of suspicion had fallen over Salinas's election. The nomination of the bookish, physically unimpressive technocrat elicited little support within the PRI's "cupola" of notables.[1]

To make matters worse, a majority of Mexicans believed that Salinas's party had stolen the 1988 presidential contest from Cuauhtémoc Cárdenas, son of former President "Tata Lázaro" Cárdenas, head of a PRI breakaway faction known as the Democratic Current and standard-bearer of a populist leftist front.[2] Even the official tally awarded Salinas but 50.7 percent of the votes cast compared to 31.06 percent for Cárdenas and 16.81 percent for the PAN nominee. This was the worst showing ever by an official party presidential candidate, who, since the mid-1960s, usually obtained 70 percent or more of the ballots cast. That almost half of the eligible voters stayed home on election day revealed both disenchantment with the political system and the fact that the PRI had lost its claim to command support of a majority of eligible voters.[3]

Salinas Seizes the Initiative

Despite an inauspicious beginning, the youthful chief executive quickly projected the image of a decisive leader in a nation that responds to strong men. Within 45 days of taking office, he had dispatched the army to arrest Joaquín "La Quina" Hernández Galicia, the supposedly "untouchable" leader of the nation's hugely wealthy and venal Oil Workers' Union. Several months later, citing corruption, he replaced Carlos Jongitud Barrios, a former governor of San Luis Potosí, who had since 1972 led the large and politically polarized

National Teachers' Union that had been one of the first groups to throw its weight behind Salinas's candidacy. Next his administration jailed Eduardo Legorreta Chauvet, a member of a powerful banking family, for manipulating securities at the time of the late 1987 stock market crash.[4]

In addition, the military captured Miguel Ángel Félix Gallardo, one of the nation's leading narcotics traffickers. Meanwhile, Treasury Secretary Pedro Aspe began to crack down on income tax evaders for the first time in modern memory. By August 1989, 79 percent of Mexicans surveyed reported a favorable image of their president.[5]

Paralleling these bold actions was Salinas's deepening of the economic "modernization" that he had championed as planning and budget secretary under de la Madrid. The president and his economic team, headed by Aspe, were determined to streamline a statist, inefficient, and corrupt economy and integrate it with the United States and Canada. Otherwise, they feared, Mexico would become a stagnant backwater as Europe and the Pacific Rim emerged as dynamic trading blocs.

In pursuit of modernization, the Salinas administration has curbed bureaucratic growth, privatized state companies, trimmed bloated subsidies, and tumbled sky-high import barriers. Further, it has slashed excessive regulations, negotiated a $4 billion annual reduction in external debt payments, courted foreign investors, and encouraged joint ventures between domestic corporations and the *ejidos.* In addition, Salinas renewed the government-labor-business "Pact for Stability and Economic Growth" (PECE), which had contributed to slashing the inflation rate from 159.2 percent in 1987 to 19.7 percent in 1989, before it climbed to 30 percent in 1990 (only to fall below 20 percent in 1991). As a result, in 1990 the GDP grew by nearly 3 percent, a figure that would surpass 4 percent in 1991.

Even while emphasizing *perestroika* at the expense of *glasnost,* Salinas also began to fulfill campaign promises to promote pluralism and fair play in Mexico's authoritarian, single-party-dominated political system. His most impressive act was defying local PRI barons to recognize the PAN's victory in the mid-1989 gubernatorial election in Baja California, a relatively prosperous state that lies cheek by jowl with the U.S. border. Salinas followed up congratulations to the *panista* governor-elect by attending his inauguration and thereby legitimizing his triumph. This conciliatory gesture set off alarms in the increasingly weakened, labor- and peasant-dominated "dinosaur" wing of the PRI that regards the opposition with all of the tenderness of a Cromwell ruling Ireland.

While building congressional coalitions with the center-right PAN on electoral reforms, the revolutionary party continued to employ political alchemy against the leftist Democratic Revolutionary Party (PRD) that embraced elements of Cárdenas's 1988 coalition.[6] Allegations of fraud marred state contests in Michoacán (July 1989), Coahuila (October 1990), and México state (November 1990). The latter, contiguous to Mexico City, received particular scrutiny because of the PRI's reported sweep of all 34 legislative seats, as well as 116 of the 121 municipalities where contests were held.

In additional bold actions, Salinas has removed 10 constitutionally elected governors, more than any president since Ruiz Cortines (1952–1958). In four of the states (Michoacán, México, Yucatán, and San Luis Potosí), governors fell because of a strong electoral showing by opposition candidates. In three cases (Baja California, Tabasco, and Jalisco), egregiously incompetent and corrupt incumbents embarrassed the administration. Ousting them served several purposes: it eliminated political liabilities, made clear to other state executives that they should act responsibly, and signaled to foreign observers that the chief executive was serious about reform.

Political Problems

The scope and velocity of Salinas's initiatives have alienated and disoriented many people. Some bureaucrats fear the loss of bribes as market forces replace Byzantine regulations. Geriatric union leaders accustomed to sweetheart contracts decry obstacles, such as tough collective bargaining, to reaping hefty salary increases and informal "commissions." Owners of small and medium-sized firms dread bankruptcy as U.S. and Japanese competitors seize more opportunities. Peasants fear displacement by machines if their communal farms are trans-

formed into capitalist enterprises under an *ejido* reform unveiled in late 1991. And intellectuals who relish yanqui-bashing lament the inexorable integration of the Mexican and U.S.
economies—a process propelled by sharply diminished protectionism and emphasis on supply-and-demand forces.

In the past, the PRI appeased, co-opted, or repressed the
discontented during periods of transition. The party's influence, however, has diminished because it has not changed
with the times. When formed in 1929, the revolutionary party
fashioned appeals to political chieftains, peasants, trade unionists, the military, and sectors of the minuscule middle class.
The past six decades have brought startling social, economic,
political, and demographic changes. Particularly impressive
has been the growth in the number of young people, city
dwellers, urban poor, bureaucrats, intellectuals, socially active
women, and members of the business community. Few of
these elements believe themselves to be represented effectively by the official party. For example, recent economic
problems have alienated the upwardly mobile middle class
whose expansion marks one of the regime's greatest
achievements.

Consequently, in 1988 Salinas finished a distant second in
Mexico City and other urban centers, and public opinion polls
revealed deep-seated cynicism and mistrust toward the party
and its leaders. Nearly half of the respondents to a mid-1989
survey expressed a belief that revolution would sweep Mexico
within five years.[7] High abstention rates plagued the 1988
national elections (50 percent) and those in 1990 in Coahuila
(75 percent) and in México state (66 percent).

Arguably, the regime survived the presidential contest in
remarkably good shape, considering the palpable disenchantment and acute economic pain that had afflicted most Mexicans under de la Madrid when the economy remained as flat as
a tortilla after the appearance of the worldwide oil glut. The
PRI managed to capture the presidency and a working legislative majority. Antifraud protesters concentrated their activities
in the Congress rather than in the streets. The police handled
those disturbances that did erupt, thereby minimizing the
civil-military confrontations that have politicized the armed

forces in traditionally democratic Venezuela and other Latin American states.

Still, the public identifies the PRI with peculation, ballot box stuffing, and political violence. Intraparty conflicts abound as old guard politicos abhor democratizing changes pushed by pro-Salinas reformers. The president's own popularity notwithstanding, only 47 percent of citizens surveyed expressed a positive view of the PRI, while 43 percent voiced negative sentiments. This figure may be low in view of the reluctance of Mexicans to criticize the system to pollsters.[8]

Overtures to the Church

In contrast to the PRI's dismal image, the Roman Catholic church wins widespread praise for its independence and sensitivity. After all, it is the only national organization that is neither funded nor controlled by the government. The people rank it with the public school system as the nation's most esteemed institution.[9] A *Nexos* magazine poll showed that 82 percent of urban Mexicans call themselves Catholics, 70.9 percent favored the pope's 1990 visit, and 68.4 percent backed civil rights for priests.[10] Support is even stronger in the countryside where priests often side with peasants against venal PRI bosses and landowners. In addition, more Mexicans are at least nominally affiliated with Catholic organizations than with labor unions, political parties, or other social and political groups.[11]

In fact, church leaders praise leading members of the Salinas administration for their commitment to Catholic values. Among the men frequently cited are Aspe, Manuel Camacho Solís (mayor of Mexico City), Jaime Serra Puche (commerce secretary), Ernesto Zedillo Ponce de León (education secretary), and Francisco Rojas (director general of Petróleos Mexicanos).[12]

As a progressive, Salinas considers anticlericalism as outmoded as a Pancho Villa mustache. Internationally, he wants to convey an image of his country as progressive and tolerant—all the better to garner loans, investment, and good will with Washington political leaders as they consider a North American Free Trade Agreement. And if the atheistic Soviet

Union can send an ambassador to the Vatican as President Gorbachev did in late 1989, why could not an overwhelmingly Catholic nation like Mexico make peace with Rome? And like any embattled politician, Salinas is on the hunt for domestic allies.

An internal PRI memorandum, circulated just before Salinas's inauguration, emphasized the potential threat posed to the government by a reinvigorated church, either acting alone or in concert with other disaffected groups. The author's style closely resembles that of Salinas's communications director, Otto Granados Roldán, who in early 1992 became the PRI's candidate for governor of Aguascalientes. The writer observed that, no longer a "precarious" institution, the church's power had "grown notably" in recent years because of several factors: its "convocatory capacity," demonstrated during the 1979 papal visit, its credibility as an institution, and its "monopoly on religious beliefs."[13]

Enhancing its strength is the church's autonomy, he argued, for it is one of the few social actors that does not depend on state subsidies. "If, indeed, the ecclesiastical hierarchy doesn't think in terms of a direct challenge as its ultimate weapon, its autonomy could permit it to conquer ever more political space and, like it or not, this would come at the expense of the state's power." It is quite possible that the church, while not attempting to displace the state, desires "better conditions for its historic regeneration."[14] Among other things, the church seeks an active role in education to exercise social control, to transmit its values, and to influence the nation's elites.[15]

The copy of the memorandum that I and at least one newspaper (*Excélsior*) obtained lacked the author's concluding pages of recommendations. Still, in the body of the text, he advocated "official flexibility by preparing public opinion . . . that the renovation and change undertaken by the current regime will necessitate reordering relations between the state and a group of social actors, including the Catholic church, without fear—this must be emphasized—of the reaction by extreme Jacobins." The change would mean virtually redefining the rules of the game, opening spaces for legitimate institutional action by diverse groups, and expanding—as a consequence of the above—the bases of support for the Institutional Revolutionary Party. It would also require reinforcing the state's role as interlocutor of diverse interests, making more transparent the state's relation with diverse groups without avoiding conflicts and without trying to deny that the intergroup interests are frequently contradictory.[16]

In pursuit of these goals, the author urged continuation of the anti-inflation PECE stability pact, with the state as its guarantor, and the dismantling of semicorporate structures such as the PRI's three sectors. "It's impossible," he argued, "to enter the twenty-first century with antiquated political and economic structures."[17]

In an apparent attempt to foster improved relations with the church, Salinas held meetings with key clerics during his campaign. Reportedly, in March 1988 he met in Chihuahua with such outspoken critics of PRI electoral practices as Archbishop Almeida (Chihuahua) and Bishops Talamás Camandari (Ciudad Juárez), Hilario Chávez Joya (Nuevo Casas Grandes), and Juan Sandoval Iñiguez (auxiliary bishop, Ciudad Juárez).[18] Long before the pope's visit was confirmed, the chief executive invited Cardinal Corripio, Archbishop Prigione, and other senior churchmen to attend his maiden address as president, the first time since the mid-nineteenth century that prelates had attended an inauguration.[19] In this speech, he said that "the modern state is that which . . . maintains openness and modernizes its relation with the church."[20] Upon leaving the ceremony, Bishop Genaro Alamilla Arteaga, president of the Episcopal Commission for Social Communications, said that, finally, "the revolution does us justice."[21]

Another example of such "justice" took place on January 26, 1989, when Salinas invited Prigione, the CEM president Suárez Rivera, and three other bishops to lunch with him at Los Pinos, his official residence. Following this meeting, which was characterized by "mutual respect," Suárez Rivera said that: "We went in through the front door . . . not through the kitchen or anything of the sort."[22] This same openness was evident four months later at Mario de Gasperín Gasperín's investiture as bishop of Querétaro. This ceremony, celebrated in the La Corregidora soccer stadium, attracted 36 bishops, 200 priests, and 35,000 laymen. The latter enlivened the festivities by sequentially jumping to their feet in "waves of faith." Obviously, such a ballyhooed event could not have occurred without the blessing of both the governor of Querétaro, Mariano Palacios Alcocer, and the government secretary.[23]

The church appeared eager to meet the government half way in improving relations. On May 31, 1989, Secretary Aspe sent an emissary to confer with 23 Mexican, U.S., and Canadian bishops attending an Inter-American Bishops Meeting in Monterrey. His objective was to obtain support from the clerics for the renegotiation of the external debt. Obligingly, the bishops made statements to the press in favor of this goal.

Then, in January 1990, the United States Bishops Conference hosted a meeting in Washington on the Mexican debt. Suárez Rivera, Corripio, and other key Mexican clerics attended, as did representatives of the government and the private sector. The 44 U.S. participants included Bernard Law, cardinal archbishop of Boston, who was born in Mexico, five other senior prelates, high government officials, members of Congress, and representatives of the banking and business community. Discussions ranged over such topics as debt-for-equity swaps, investment, access to the U.S. market, and development assistance. The North American bishops, however, captured the moral tenor of the sessions when they presented a document containing a letter sent to President George Bush. Their communication stated, in part, that

> we feel profoundly anguished by the destructive effects of the debt on the real population, especially the poor of the world, who had no part in creating the debt and who received minimal benefits from it. Mexico has acted quite responsibly in adopting necessary measures to reorganize its economy. But in so doing, the people's standard of living has suffered hugely. Even so, Mexico has not been able to reduce its debt; to the contrary, the debt has risen. Moreover, this effort [to pay its obligations] is strangling its economy.[24]

The bishops added that: "The debt problem with its human consequences is economically unsustainable, politically dangerous and ethically unacceptable."[25]

Father Enrique González Torres used the Washington conference as a forum to promote the church's version of debt-for-equity swaps. The Jesuit, scion of an entrepreneurial family, heads the Foundation for Assistance to the Community (FAC), formed to distribute aid from Catholic Relief Services and other international humanitarian assistance in the wake of the devastating earthquakes of September 1985. By April 1986, FAC had spent more than 217 million pesos in Mexico City, Jalisco, and Michoacán.

Since then, with the cooperation of the Mexican government and U.S. Catholic prelates and lay people, González Torres has pursued the purchase of discounted Mexican debt and its conversion into pesos. He has used these monies to construct housing, supply food to the hungry, train workers, and fund other social projects. Although he denies blatant political motives, Archbishop Suárez Rivera admits that the FAC venture demonstrates a good faith effort by the church to show both social responsibility and its readiness to cooperate with the government "for the benefit of all the people."[26]

The Episcopal Conferences of Mexico, the United States, and Canada also expressed themselves on the proposed Free Trade Agreement. Any such accord, they insisted, "must not forget to initiate actions" to uplift the poor, safeguard small and medium-sized industries, and protect "the environment, culture, and truth."[27]

In keeping with the atmosphere of conciliation, Salinas announced in February 1990 the selection of Agustín Téllez Cruces as his "personal envoy" to the Vatican. Other presidents had designated informal representatives to the church. Benigno Ugarte, a lawyer from Morelos who enjoyed close ties to Archbishop Martínez, discharged this function under Cárdenas and Avila Camacho; later, attorney Jorge Martínez y Gómez del Campo, a friend of Archbishop Dario Miranda y Gomez, served in this role for Echeverría and López Portillo. Martínez y Gómez, who took advantage of his position to acquire a minor government post, even wanted to organize a special office to deal with church-state relations.[28]

The selection of Ugarte and Martínez received little publicity compared to that lavished on Salinas's selection of Téllez

Cruces. In contrast to his predecessors, the 73-year-old Téllez Cruces commands national prominence, having served as president of the Supreme Court of Justice, federal senator, and interim governor of Guanajuato.

Papal Visit

At first blush, the pope's 1990 visit appeared similar to the one 11 years before. Both involved massive, enthusiastic crowds, dawn to dusk television coverage, crass media advertising by banks and other enterprises, and government-provided transportation, security, and equipment without which neither visit would have been possible. Still, there were significant differences. To begin with, 1978 was the "year of three popes," and the Vatican was beset by change and uncertainty, with John Paul being elevated in October. Thus, the Mexican church and government had only a few weeks to lay plans for John Paul II's visit in January 1979. At the end of 1978, a Foreign Ministry spokesman issued a statement, saying: "The pope has made no request for a visa, if he files an application, it will be handled like that of any other tourist."[29] Although the government began to mobilize resources once the visit was confirmed, it was far more "improvised and spontaneous" than the second, for which the hosts had several months during which to make preparations.[30]

More significant than timing and logistics were dissimilarities in presidential behavior. According to a senior Mexican cleric, López Portillo professed to have lost his faith in God upon reading Marx and Lenin at age 15. While claiming to follow "Christian morality" and having a child married at a mass at Los Pinos, he practiced no religion.[31] In his memoirs, the former president stated that, upon ceasing to believe in and to practice Catholicism, he embraced "the ideology of the Mexican Revolution."[32]

López Portillo engaged in a charade to persuade the public that he and the pope had met by chance at Mexico City's Benito Juárez Airport, an ironic name for a facility that would receive the first papal visit to Mexico. According to one possibly apocryphal account, the game found the president flying over the capital in his helicopter, landing only after the pontiff's airplane reached the tarmac. Then López Portillo, accompanied by his wife and one aide, proffered but a perfunctory handshake and a few vapid words of welcome before disappearing into his limousine and speeding off. Reportedly, even these insipid gestures excited criticism from Masonic lodges.[33] Yet, when these latter-day Jacobins complained that the visitor violated the Mexican constitution by wearing his papal garments in public, López Portillo ridiculed the critics by offering to pay the 50-peso fine.

As mentioned in chapter 2, Salinas is not a practicing Catholic. Initially, he, too, was reluctant to greet the Holy Father upon his arrival. His misgivings were dispelled by arguments advanced by Prigione and José María Córdoba Montoya, the president's chief of staff and a key adviser, that his presence at the airport would benefit his administration.[34] Thus, Salinas, acting in a "strictly personal" capacity but surrounded by an entourage of public officials, warmly welcomed the "pilgrim of peace" once his plane touched down on May 6.

In addition, the youthful chief executive praised the pope for promoting "more justice, more participation, more attentiveness, especially by those who have less because their future is also ours." "Your Holiness," he added, "your return inspires a warm and beautiful reminder of your previous visit, as well as of the humane cause of peace and, today in Mexico, of solidarity."[35] Salinas's airport welcome, to which more than 90 percent of all television sets were tuned, raised the president's popularity 4 to 6 percentage points.[36] Enhancing the media attention was the fact that six times as many journalists (600) covered the 1990 visit compared to 1979.[37]

Salinas shrewdly involved the Holy Father in legitimizing the National Solidarity Program (PRONASOL), his administration's most ambitious attempt to excite local support by providing federal funds for social projects in which communities invest sweat capital, in-kind resources, and locally generated monies. On his second day in Mexico, John Paul II celebrated a mass in Chalco, a sprawling México state shantytown whose 500,000 inhabitants have been a showcase for PRONASOL experiments. "I exhort Christians and all men of good will in Mexico," he said, "to reawaken a social conscience of solidarity."[38]

Salinas elicited the pope's blessing for a program that improved the chief executive's legitimacy with the poor, especially slum dwellers and campesinos. PRONASOL ameliorates harsh social conditions, projects a reformist image for his government, and invites favorable comparisons to Poland's Solidarity Movement. By circumventing entrenched state and local politicians, the program facilitates penetration of a relatively unorganized segment of the population by presidential emissaries, who in some areas constitute a political organization parallel to the PRI. The initiative identifies and recruits authentic community leaders and links them to the government, thereby focusing them on constructive goals that buttress rather than challenge the official party's hegemonic status. That they set priorities for their communities enhances the stake that grass-roots leaders have in the success of local ventures. Prigione praised Solidarity as "a really good program that deserves to be backed [because] it invites the people to get involved, requires their involvement."[39] The government will erect an "Urban Solidarity Center," including a chapel, on the site in Chalco where the pope offered a mass that attracted several million people.

While vexing to PRI hacks because the program was independent of their party, PRONASOL impedes the progress of opposition parties in areas where their candidates ran well in 1988. The success of the program, to which the government committed more than $1.67 billion in resources in 1991, helps explain the PRI's unusually modest recourse to fraud, except in Guanajuato state, where it obtained 61.4 percent of the vote in the August 1991 congressional elections.[40]

In 1979 most public figures followed López Portillo's example and remained aloof from the pope during his five days in their country. In 1990 cabinet members and elected officials, including governors of the 10 states on the Bishop of Rome's itinerary, also took a cue from their *jefe máximo* and openly and heartily greeted John Paul II. An unabashed Catholic, the governor of Chihuahua, Fernando Baeza Meléndez, went so far as to kiss the hierarch's ring. In mid-1991, a crowd of 3,000 applauded Baeza when he and his wife received communion at the mass celebrating the investiture of the new bishop of Chihuahua. Governors and mayors throughout the country have been less demonstrative than Baeza, but they have initiated or increased contacts with local church leaders.

Moreover, in 1979 television cameras zeroed in on the pope, his motorcade, his airplane's landings and take-offs—only to pan faces in the crowd when he offered homilies or other religious messages.[41] Eleven years later, such utterances received full attention along with the pontiff's movement through an enormous sea of humanity. Although some 15 million Mexicans saw John Paul II in 1979, civil and clerical authorities estimated that approximately 30 to 40 million people observed him during his longer 1990 visit.[42] This turn-out is all the more remarkable because popes usually attract smaller crowds the second time they visit a country.[43]

The Self-Destructive Left

Cárdenas, his Democratic Revolutionary Party (PRD), and other leftist groups had a golden opportunity to take political advantage of the papal visit. Although his criticism of the economic and political establishment was not as trenchant as in 1979, the pope did illuminate the plight of Mexico's "have-nots." Some observers claim that he did not exhibit as much passion on social issues as in 1979.[44] Still, the Holy Father excoriated bureaucratic corruption, illiteracy, unemployment, family disintegration, low salaries, inflation, the economic crisis, and hunger and malnutrition in a country in which at least one-third of the population goes to bed hungry each night. In addition, he lamented the concentration of wealth in the hands of the few and scolded affluent entrepreneurs for doing so little to uplift the poor who lived as ragpickers in fetid slums. John Paul II rebuffed cattlemen who implored him to rein in liberationist priests and other progressives fighting for campesino rights. He told them in no uncertain terms that communism's collapse in Eastern Europe did not vindicate liberal capitalism as the only acceptable economic system.[45]

In what appeared as an attack on government policy, he stated: "We expected a more just world; that a de facto democracy would become a bastion of human rights; that economic development would not be achieved by sacrificing the smaller and weaker; and that technical and scientific progress would make us happier."[46] In addition, the pope expressed to an assembly of diplomats the "urgency" of resolving the Latin American debt crisis, which "has become a burden and, in some cases . . . it has even accentuated underdevelopment." The pontiff advocated placing value on the "ethical dimension" of the economic suffering caused by the foreign debt—which in Mexico surpasses $92 billion—and recommended regional solidarity to confront the problem.[47]

Virtually every papal pronouncement offered ammunition to Cárdenas and his colleagues, who declaim their commitment to "workers, peasants, slum-dwellers, and the dispossessed." The PRD and its cohorts might have been expected to wrap themselves in the pope's speeches, while excoriating Salinas's neoliberal government for stressing debt repayments, market mechanisms, and preference for the private sector at the expense of those who eke out a living at the bottom of a distended social pyramid.

Instead of making common cause with John Paul II, however, Cárdenas criticized both the "squandering" of resources on the visit and the pope's meddling in Mexican politics by seeking constitutional reforms.[48] In a similar vein, Francisco Ortiz Mendoza, head of the Popular Socialist Party (PPS) that backed Cárdenas's 1988 presidential bid, expressed "disgust" at the papal visit and the friendly attitude of state governors toward their guest. Reportedly, Ortiz Mendoza had urged the application of the constitution's Article 33 to remove the pope from the country. In any case, he stated a readiness to sue the state officials who had greeted the visitor so warmly.[49] These comments served as a prelude to a demand, made by PPS Deputy Marcela Lombardo in 1991, that Apostolic Delegate Prigione be dismissed from the country for interfering in local politics.[50]

Why did TELEVISA, the state-influenced TV network, so fully ventilate this carping by dissidents, who usually receive short shrift from the media conglomerate? One explanation lies in the quantity of airtime that had to be filled during eight days of extensive coverage. Yet, the more compelling reason was an eagerness to allow the Left to hang itself with the rope of anticlericalism. By pope-bashing, Cárdenas, Ortiz Mendoza, and their colleagues demonstrated their insensitivity to grass-roots interests in one of world's most Catholic countries, where the overwhelming majority of the population embraces the faith. As Sergio Sarmiento, a writer for the daily *El Financiero*, stated: "Rather than pay attention [to the public's veneration of the pope] . . . the left preferred to stir up old dogmas that insist that religion is the opiate of the people."[51]

Even as detractors were lambasting the Holy Father, on the eve of his departure Salinas personally bade him farewell on the red phone that the president had given the apostolic delegate to facilitate church-state communication.[52]

During his mid-1991 visit to Europe, the president was received by the pope in a special audience that was highly publicized by Mexico's print and electronic media. John Paul II praised the Salinas administration for promoting "solidarity" and social justice at home, seeking to resolve the violence and conflict besetting Central America, and fostering a climate propitious to dialogue and understanding between Mexico's civil and church authorities. On the latter point, he emphasized: "In a state based on law, the full recognition of religious liberty is, at once, the fruit and guarantee of other civil liberties." In response, Salinas recommended neither the modification of the 1917 Constitution nor the establishment of diplomatic relations between Mexico and the Vatican. He did, however, reiterate his commitment to "modernizing the economic, political, and social life of the nation."[53] He also presented his host with an eighteenth-century painting of the Virgin of Guadalupe. Even a few years ago such a gift would have aroused severe political attacks on any Mexican politician.

Human Rights and Other Reforms

In May 1990, during a two-hour "respectful and cordial" meeting with Salinas at Los Pinos, John Paul II showed great tact in not raising questions about the legal status of the church in Mexico. Instead, the two men discussed changes in Eastern Europe, the need to strengthen solidarity to eliminate the dangers of individualism and consumerism, and the "lack of faith worldwide."[54] Nonetheless, encouraged by the pontiff's popularity in Mexico, the Mexican Catholic leaders continued to press for legal reforms. They crystallized their goals in a detailed communiqué directed to Salinas by the CEM Presidency in mid-1989 and reissued in 1990.

Entitled *Church-State Relations,* this memorandum reflected the astute draftsmanship of Bishop Reynoso Cervantes, judicial adviser to Archbishop Suárez Rivera. The author reiterated the need to "modernize" relations between the government and churches, thereby hurling back at Salinas the widely quoted phrase employed in his initial speech as chief executive. He emphasized how drastically conditions had changed since 1917, the fact that worshipers openly flouted the prohibitions on public religious services, and that such behavior undermined the regime's substantive as opposed to formal legitimacy. To add insult to injury, the Constitution violated such accords subscribed to by Mexico as the International Pact of Political and Civil Rights, the American Declaration of Rights and Duties of Man, and the American Convention on Human Rights.

The bishops followed this indictment with projected amendments to Articles 3, 5, 24, 27, and 130 of the fundamental law. They advocated, inter alia, allowing private schools, with official authorization, at all levels; granting academic freedom to universities; respecting fully individual freedom; permitting churches and social welfare institutions to acquire property compatible with their goals; and revising Article 130 with language similar to the religion clause in the First Amendment of the U.S. Constitution. The latter proclaimed church-state separation and religious freedom and prohibited Congress from establishing or banning any religion. "The proposed text," according to the prelates, "will open new horizons in relations between the State and churches, principally the Catholic Church, for the benefit of the Mexican society whose progress will be advanced; it will maintain . . . the nature and reciprocal respect of state and ecclesiastical entities, as well as noninterference in their respective domains: the civil-temporal and the religious-spiritual."[55]

Even as the apostolic delegate, Cardinal Corripio, and the CEM president persistently and diplomatically made their case for amendments (in 1990 and 1991, Prigione held meetings with congressional leaders in the Apostolic Delegation), certain Jesuits showed less discretion as they castigated the PRI for human rights abuses. Most outspoken has been Father Jesús Maldonado of the Miguel Agustín Pro Center, a think tank named for a priest martyred during the *Cristero* rebellion.

In early 1990, the Center issued *La situación de los derechos humanos en méxico durante 1989,* a document that asserted that human rights abuses had increased during the first year of Salinas's administration. "The democratic advances registered thus far reflect only a representative democracy controlled by the PRI and the government; it is a long way from satisfying popular democratic demands that seek effective participation in the fundamental decisions of the country: political, economic, national sovereignty, etc." The Jesuits discounted the PAN victory in Baja California because of the widespread repression of Cárdenas's PRD, a party that offers an alternative to Salinas's economic and political goals. "It might be said that the government is prepared to recognize only those opponents who do not differ with the fundamentals of its program."[56] In describing the 1989 Michoacán elections, the Jesuits emphasized "the climate of tension and intimidation of the people by the presence of the army and different police agencies; irregularities in the electoral rolls; massive aggression; arbitrary detentions; multiple voting; and the stealing and burning of ballot boxes."[57]

Needless to say, the Society of Jesus is not monolithic, as evidenced by Father González Torres's attempts, manifest at the January 1990 debt conference in Washington, to promote church-state accommodation.

On the heels of the papal visit, Salinas established a National Human Rights Commission (CNDH), prompted by a series of political killings, most notably that of Norma Corona Sapienz, who headed Sinaloa state's human rights commission. She had accused the Federal Judicial Police in Sinaloa of criminal activity while they persecuted alleged drug traffickers. Also damning were statistics published by the Latin American Federation of Journalists that showed Mexico third (55) after Argentina (113) and Guatemala (70) in the number of journalists murdered over the past 20 years.[58]

Its inability to launch investigations without a formal complaint limits the Commission's powers. Still, some 800 allegations to the CNDH of flagrant abuses by the antinarcotics squad of the Federal Judicial Police sparked the removal in October 1990 of Javier Coello Trejo as drug czar and deputy attorney general. Upon the recommendation of the Commission, the National Defense Secretariat began legal proceedings against six army officers implicated in a drug-trafficking shoot-out in which two Federal Judicial policemen died in November 1991. Earlier that year the head of the CNDH urged the church to become even more involved in advancing human rights.[59]

The chief executive's mid-1990 creation of the CNDH preceded, by only a few days, a report issued by Americas Watch. In its 115-page study, the New York-based human rights organization compiled an alarming inventory of violations, including torture and mistreatment of prisoners, extrajudicial killings, wholesale denial of due process rights, recourse to violence in resolving agrarian disputes, harassment of independent trade unions, and violations of press freedom.[60] Whether the report and the contemporaneous rash of criticism will do any good remains to be seen. Although Mexico is acutely sensitive to outside criticism, the Americas Watch report emphasized that "rather than moving toward improvements in human rights conditions, Mexico may be heading for a period of increased violent abuses and suppression of dissent."[61]

The CEM's Permanent Council took advantage of the pope's successful visit and the prevailing climate for human rights reform to renew its quest for "the right to religious freedom." In a statement published in the daily newspaper *Excélsior*, the Council stressed that respect for human rights, which are natural rights anterior to the formation of nations, constitute a "valid criterion" for judging a country's level of civilization and quality of culture. Further, the bishops argued that the peace and harmony of citizens and the authentic progress of peoples depends on a regime's respect for these rights. "The human experience demonstrates that, when a government ignores, impedes or violates these fundamental rights, be it in legislation or in daily life, it is heading for totalitarianism." The document concluded by emphasizing that religious liberty was "fundamental" to man's other rights. While applauding the formation of the human rights commission, the churchmen expressed hope that "these rights [will] be fully recognized and better expressed in legislation, as well as promoted and respected with greater zeal and efficiency in the life of all Mexicans."[62]

Conclusion

In his state-of-the-nation address on November 1, 1991, President Salinas answered the bishops' prayers by announcing his intention to normalize the government's relations with the church. Amid prolonged applause he stated:

> Based on experience, the Mexican people do not want the clergy taking part in politics or amassing material wealth. The people, however, do not want to live a pretense or misguided complicity. The idea is not to return to existence of privilege, but to reconcile the definite secularization of our society with effective freedom of beliefs, something that constitutes one of the most important human rights.[63]

Subsequently, he proposed a "new legal status of the church" by amending Articles 3, 5, 24, 27, and 130 of the fundamental law. These changes recognize churches of all faiths as legal entities and permit them to own property. Convents and monasteries that operated in defiance of constitutional prohibitions will be allowed to exist legally. Their buildings will be owned by the government; yet any new churches or synagogues that are constructed will belong to the organizations that build them. The reform legalizes the presence of foreign priests and ministers in Mexico. The clergy will also have the right to vote and criticize the government, while religious bodies will be permitted to publish newspapers and disseminate their beliefs on television and radio stations. Religious officials will be required to pay taxes on any income that they earn.

On December 18, 1991, after 25 hours of debate, the Chamber of Deputies endorsed the reforms by a vote of 380 to 22, thus paving the way for approval by the Senate and state legislatures. Only the Popular Socialist Party opposed the changes, and some of its members shouted ¡Viva Benito Juárez! when the tally was announced. "After so many years of incomprehension, of struggles, of suffering and frustration between the state and the churches, we have reached an opening," stated Archbishop Prigione.[64]

Not everyone shared Prigione's enthusiasm. Some Protestant leaders feared that the government would favor the Catholic church over their denominations and sects. Mainstream Protestant faiths and evangelicals have gained hundreds of thousands of adherents in recent years. As mentioned above, the evangelicals have made impressive strides in the South, thanks in part to their extraordinary vitality in Guatemala where the president, Jorge Antonio Serrano Elías, is a conservative businessman and Christian evangelical.

Even elements within the Roman Catholic community expressed misgivings about how negotiations between clerical and civil authorities were conducted. Most outspoken was the Conference of Religious Institutes of Mexico, dominated by the Jesuits, the Franciscans, the Dominicans, the Benedictines, and the Salesians. In an internal document that was leaked to the press, the CIRM lamented that the church-state reconciliation had involved only the "cupolas" of the government and the CEM. "It's unfortunate that the Catholic hierarchy appears to have largely ignored the rest of the Catholics: it neither considered if these relations would benefit the people, nor asked their opinion," according to the memorandum.

The CIRM worried that a "reprivatized" or co-opted church would confer legitimacy on the neo-liberal economic policies of a government that impeded democratization. Now that it enjoyed a legal status, might not the church emphasize its private schools and universities and its ministry to the power elite, while neglecting its commitment to workers, peasants, and the poor? "The Church thus reprivatized engages in even less social confrontation," averred the CIRM document, "than a Church that, despite the lack of juridical recognition, enjoyed an exceptional and privileged freedom in a de facto sense."[65]

On February 14, 1992, less than two weeks after the publication of the CIRM memorandum, the CEM hierarchy denounced the document in an advertisement in *Excélsior*. The bishops dismissed the CIRM leadership as "a small group" who erroneously believed that it spoke for all religious in Mexico and sought to establish a parallel magisterium or teaching authority. They condemned the communiqué as "false, unjust and calumnious," claimed the pope's backing for the episcopate's position vis-à-vis the government, and emphasized that it was the bishops—not the CIRM and its affiliates—who had the obligation to instruct the Catholic faithful. "We reiterate our preferential option for the poor and insist that the constitutional reforms not only do not impede this commitment but facilitate it."[66]

The Vatican manifested its support for developments in Mexico by accelerating the process of beatification of 26 Mexicans, 25 of whom were martyred during the *Cristero* rebellion. In addition, Foreign Secretary Fernando Solano Morales expressed his belief that diplomatic relations, severed in 1857, would be renewed between Mexico and the Holy See after the constitutional amendments had been adopted.[67] A crucial step toward this renewal will take place during John Paul II's projected visit to Yucatan in October 1992.

What are the prospects for church-state relations in Mexico?

1. As a consequence of its recognition by the government, the church will occupy more political space. Its influence may prove greatest in the struggle for human rights—an issue that both commands saliency across the spectrum of Roman Catholics and attracts attention from domestic and foreign publics. The church can be expected to encourage the activities of the National Human Rights Commission. The many local church leaders inspired by liberation theology are likely to agitate, with growing militancy, if the PRI reneges on its promise to complement economic reforms with greater social justice.

In March 1992, for instance, Dominican and Jesuit priests joined some 300 Indians (Tzeltales, Choles, Tzotziles, and Zoques) in a march from Palenque, the heart of the Maya region of Chiapas, to Mexico City to protest police repression, land seizures, and other human rights violations. Dominican priest Gonzalo Ituarte, secretary of the diocese of San Cristóbal de las Casas, said that "if the people scream [against injustices], we must be their sound box."[68] And the CIRM's rank and file will cross swords with the CEM if the latter emphasizes such political aspects of human rights as electoral reform rather than raising the banner of the nation's poor and downtrodden. The PRI regime's presence as a declared "enemy" engendered a certain degree of unity within a heterogenous church. Removal of the external threat may foreshadow more intramural conflicts.

2. Mexico's quest to integrate its economy with the United States and Canada will provide an additional impulse to improving human rights. After all, abuses attributed to Mexican officials show up on prime time U.S. television broadcasts and on the cover of *Time* and *Newsweek* magazines. In stressing Mexico's legal commitment to civil liberties through the conventions and treaties it has signed, bishops north and south of the Rio Grande have already taken advantage of the international dimension of this question. The drive toward economic integration will inspire more cooperative ventures among U.S., Canadian, and Mexican bishops. This collaboration represents an expansion and institutionalization of meetings held for many years by prelates in states on both sides of the U.S. and Mexican border. The 1990 Washington debt meeting was a harbinger of greater bilateral cooperation on such vital concerns as economics, narcotics, immigration, and trade. In its wake, North American bishops have insisted, for example, that any free-trade pact contain safeguards against the exploitation and displacement of workers and farmers unable to protect their own interests. These prelates will speak out even more on human rights matters in the United States, particularly abuses suffered by legal and illegal Mexican workers. It remains to be seen whether Protestant denominations will nurture similar linkages and express their views on broader policy questions. Still, a number of Canadian churches (Roman Catholics, Presbyterian, Anglican, Quaker, Reformed, and evangelical) have insisted that Prime Minister Brian Mulroney refuse to sign a NAFTA agreement should the Salinas government fail to act decisively on human rights abuses.[69]

3. Eventually, domestic reforms and increased continental economic ties should ameliorate the conditions suffered by poorer Mexicans who operate within the mainstream

economy—an objective shared by clerics and politicians. In the short to medium term, however, integration will actually displace many of these workers, especially in such *ejido*-infested regions as the South that depend heavily on agriculture and can expect few benefits from the NAFTA. Ministering to the needs of these workers, as well as to the one-third of Mexicans who eke out a living at the margin of the cash economy, could exacerbate tensions between adherents of liberation theology and traditionalists within the Roman Catholic church; it could also sharpen the antagonism between Catholic social activists and the government, as well as between Catholics and the better-funded fundamentalist Protestant missionaries. The latter, encouraged by the attention lavished on Mexico in recent years, are flocking to the country in ever larger numbers.

4. Although Pope John Paul II blessed the Solidarity initiative at Chalco and Salinas has extended a pro forma invitation, the government has not vigorously encouraged church participation in this program. Consequently, the church's involvement has been limited to a handful of projects. As PRONASOL expands in importance and visibility, it is likely that the church will seek an active role in the program to advance its own social mission. In fact, Solidarity may provide opportunities for priests, socially aware laymen, and religious brothers and sisters animated by liberation theology to work with both the poor and with government officials. Under such conditions, the Marxist trappings of liberation theology might be shed in favor of Peace Corps-type involvement. Such church activism will not immunize PRONASOL against accusations that it is a political instrument of the PRI—a charge that gained credibility during the 1992 gubernatorial campaigns. Still, the church's involvement will underscore the pluralism of the program and its contribution to improving social conditions. In the past, ambitious, highly publicized community development programs failed to survive beyond the terms of the chief executives who inspired them. Church participation, along with the elevation of the Solidarity program to cabinet status, should help ensure PRONASOL's continuation into the administration of Salinas's successor.

5. NAFTA-inspired development will promote materialistic and consumer values in Mexico that are inimical to the professed Roman Catholic social doctrine. Modernization may also reduce the number of religious vocations in the country, a problem afflicting the church in the United States, Western Europe, and other developed areas. Meanwhile, the number of Protestant ministers, particularly in the ranks of the evangelical churches, will grow because of the modest educational requirements for ordination and the right they have to marry. If, emboldened by their success in Guatemala, the evangelicals eventually strive for an organized role in Mexican politics, they can expect resistance, perhaps even repression, at the hands of the government.

6. NAFTA will raise the salience of the birth control issue. As many deracinated Mexican peasants and workers emigrate northward in quest of a better life, this continued diaspora of illegal aliens will elicit cries of protest, foreshadowed in Patrick J. Buchanan's platform for the Republican nomination for president in 1992 and from some U.S. and Canadian opinion leaders who want more rigorous border management. That one-third of the alleged looters arrested during the April 1992 Los Angeles disturbances were unlawful immigrants, mainly from Mexico, will amplify this appeal. Other politicians may demand that Mexico reduce its birthrate even lower. Pressure will mount to decriminalize abortions, a reform favored by a growing number of politically aware Mexican women whose cause may be embraced by their U.S. and Canadian counterparts. The CEM is counting on the PRI to thwart such changes in the future, just as the party has done in the past. Birth control is a highly sensitive issue in Mexico, and external comments on this policy will raise nationalistic hackles and help the bishops impede changes.

7. In view of Pope John Paul II's emphatic enthusiasm for Salinas, political pragmatists in the hierarchy will spurn support for the PAN in favor of accommodating a PRI administration that has done more than any of its predecessors to champion church-state rapprochement. Contributing to this "hands off" strategy is the PRI's cultivation of the PAN to create parliamentary coalitions to pass electoral, banking, and *ejido* legislation, Salinas's recognition of the PAN's gubernato-

rial victory in Baja California, the willingness of the government to void gubernatorial elections in Guanajuato and San Luis Potosí in the face of *panista* protests in 1991, and the PRI's recruitment of pro-business candidates for the governorships of Chihuahua and Michoacán in 1992. Nothing will prevent ecclesiastical authorities from criticizing such corrupt institutions as certain affiliates of the Confederation of Mexican Workers, a long-time and bitter antagonist of the Catholic church. Nor will the northern bishops refrain from excoriating rigged elections and other electoral abuses: to remain silent would contravene their beliefs and jeopardize the loyalty of their followers.

8. The end of the cold war and the dismantling of East European Communist regimes will diminish the already anemic following of TECOS, MURO, and other extreme right-wing groups that strive to articulate pre-Vatican II Catholic values. Also lessening their appeal is the sagging strength of the domestic Left, a target of propaganda and mobilization drives by the Catholic Right. At the same time, greater emphasis on free enterprise and the burgeoning role of the private sector provide a climate favorable to the growth of Opus Dei. Now confined largely to entrepreneurial activities, Opus Dei may seek in Mexico, as it has elsewhere in Latin America, greater political influence. Rather than launch a new party or resuscitate the moribund Mexican Democratic Party, Opus Dei could expand its presence within the PAN and even forge links with the profoundly pragmatic PRI.

9. Salinas's remarkably well-received overtures toward the church should broaden his party's appeal in the 1994 presidential election. The president's deft action has identified the PRI with a popular cause, thus robbing the PAN (which has already lost the economic liberalization mantle) of yet one more issue and making the PRD (which begrudgingly backed the constitutional reform) appear increasingly out of touch with mass sentiments. Particularly well positioned to take advantage of the church-state reconciliation are such leading candidates for the PRI nomination as Pedro Aspe, Manuel Camacho Solís, and Ernesto Zedillo Ponce de Léon, whom key churchmen praise for leading lives inspired by church teachings.

10. As noted, Salinas's modernization program will produce significant dislocations and hardships before robust, sustained economic growth occurs. Symbolic appeals to Catholics may help to mitigate the discontent. The Virgin of Guadalupe transcends the red, white, and green national flag as a symbol of national unity. After all, even revered figures like Hidalgo, Juárez, and Lázaro Cárdenas pale in comparison to the miraculous madonna. By extending the olive branch to the church, Salinas may buy time for his version of *perestroika* to bear fruit and still avoid the upheaval that has beset other nations whose leaders have neglected or disdained traditional institutions as they sought to propel their countries from backwardness into the First World.

Notes

Chapter 1

1. Jean A. Meyer, *The Cristero Rebellion: The Mexican People between Church and State 1926–1929* (London: Cambridge University Press, 1976), 1.

2. Catholic University of America, *New Catholic Encyclopedia,* vol. 9 (Palatine, Ill.: Jack Heraty and Associates, 1981), 771.

3. Frank Tannenbaum, *Mexico: The Struggle for Peace and Bread* (New York: Columbia University Press, 1950), 126.

4. Michael C. Meyer and William L. Sherman, *The Course of Mexican History*, 3rd ed. (New York: Oxford University Press, 1987), 189.

5. Ibid., 188.

6. Hugh Thomas, "The Mexican Labyrinth," a study prepared for the Twentieth Century Fund, New York, November 1990, p. 14.

7. Alexander von Humboldt, *Ensayo político sobre la nueva-españa,* vol. 1 (Paris, 1821), 112.

8. J. Lloyd Mecham, *Church and State in Latin America* (Chapel Hill: University of North Carolina Press, 1934), 42.

9. *New Catholic Encyclopedia,* vol. 9, p. 773.

10. Jan Bazant, *A Concise History of Mexico: From Hidalgo to Cárdenas, 1805–1940* (New York: Cambridge University Press, 1977), 6.

11. Meyer and Sherman, *The Course of Mexican History,* 279.

12. Bazant, *A Concise History of Mexico,* 7.

13. Meyer and Sherman, *The Course of Mexican History,* 288.

14. Mecham, *Church and State in Latin America,* 65.

15. Claude Pomerleau, "The Changing Church in Mexico and Its Challenge to the State," *Review of Politics* 43 (October 1981): 542.

16. Mecham, *Church and State in Latin America,* 424.

17. *New Catholic Encyclopedia,* vol. 9, p. 779.

18. Thomas, "The Mexican Labyrinth," 16.

19. Ibid., 259.

20. Donald J. Mabry, *Mexico's Acción Nacional: A Catholic Alternative to Revolution* (Syracuse: Syracuse University Press, 1973), 17.

21. Quoted in Manuel Olímon Nolasco, "Iglesia y estado ¿Por que el miedo a los cambios?" in José Trinidad González R., ed., *Relaciones iglesia-estado en méxico* (Mexico City: Librería Parroquial de Clavería, S. A. de C. V., 1990), 39.

22. *Constitución política de los estados unidos mexicanos* (Mexico City: Editorial Teocalli, 1976). Nowhere in the text are there specific references to the Roman Catholic church; all references to church are either in the plural or generic.

23. *New York Times,* June 22, 1929, p. 2.

24. Mabry, *Mexico's Acción Nacional,* 18–19.

25. Claudia Carlen, *The Papal Encyclicals 1903–1939* (Raleigh, N.C.: McGrath Publishing Co., 1981), 305.

26. Meyer, *The Cristero Rebellion,* 18.

27. *New York Times,* June 26, 1929, p. 2.

28. Ibid., June 23, 1929, pp. 1–2.

29. Roderic Ai Camp, "Religious Elites in Mexico—Some Preliminary Observations," a paper presented at XV International Congress of the Latin American Studies Association, Miami, Florida, December 1989 (mimeo.), 4.

30. *New York Times,* December 6, 1933, p. 13.

31. Ibid., December 14, 1931, p. 10.

32. The encyclical's full text appears in Carlen, *The Papal Encyclicals 1903–1939,* pp. 305–312.

33. Ibid., 489.

34. *New York Times,* October 3, 1932, p. 6; and October 4, 1932, p. 7.

35. Ibid., October 31, 1934, p. 1.

36. Ibid., January 26, 1935, p. 14.

37. Thomas, "The Mexican Labyrinth," 75.

38. Ibid.

39. *New York Times,* March 30, 1937, p. 22.

40. Ibid., May 3, 1938, p. 12.

41. Alan Knight, *United States and Mexico* (San Diego: Center for U.S. and Mexican Studies, 1987), 51.

42. Howard F. Cline, *The United States and Mexico,* rev. ed. (New York: Atheneum, 1965), 294.

43. Thomas, "The Mexican Labyrinth," 87.

44. Although dated, the most comprehensive book on the PAN remains Mabry's *Mexico's Acción National;* see, in particular, pp. 32–49.

45. Thomas, "The Mexican Labyrinth," 71.

46. Ibid., 89.

47. David C. Bailey, "The Church since 1940," in W. Dirk Raat and William H. Beezley, eds., *Twentieth-Century Mexico* (Lincoln: University of Nebraska Press, 1986), 237–238.

48. Ibid., 238.

49. *El Financiero,* June 14, 1991, p. 36.

50. *New York Times,* December 20, 1991, p. A–15.

51. Ibid., October 12, 1942, p. 5.

52. Ibid., February 20, 1952, p. 12.

53. Ibid., December 4, 1959, p. 2.

54. Soledad Loaeza-Lajous, "Continuity and Change in the Mexican Catholic Church," in Dermot Keogh, ed., *Church and Politics in Latin America* (London: Macmillan, 1990), 285.

Chapter 2

1. Conferencia del Episcopado Mexicano, *Directorio 1989/ 1991* (Mexico City: CEM, 1990), 16.

2. Genaro Alamilla Arteaga, bishop emeritus of Papantla, is still considered active and enjoys a vote in plenary assemblies because he is president of the Episcopal Commission on Social Communications. A bishop emeritus is considered active if he holds a post with the Vatican, the Conference of Mexican Bishops, or the Latin American Episcopal Conference known as CELAM, an organization discussed below.

3. Even if they serve two consecutive terms, members of the Presidency may, after a lapse of three years, seek reelection. For example, the Plenary Assembly elected Archbishop Ernesto Corripio Ahumada president for the period February 1968 to October 1973 and again from December 1979 to November 1982 (by which time he was a cardinal).

4. CEM, *Directorio 1989/1991,* 19.

5. Ibid., 24.

6. Ibid., 26.

7. Ibid.

8. Felician A. Foy, ed., *1992 Catholic Almanac* (Huntington, Ind.: Our Sunday Visitor, Inc., 1991).

9. Felician A. Foy, ed., *1990 Catholic Almanac* (Huntington, Ind.: Our Sunday Visitor, Inc., 1989).

10. Phillip Berryman, "Basic Christian Communities and the Future of Latin America," *Monthly Review* 36 (July–August 1984): 27.

11. *A Theology of Liberation* (Maryknoll, N.Y.: Orbis, 1973).

12. Denis Goulet, "The Mexican Church: Into the Public Arena," *America* 60 (April 8, 1989): 322.

13. Ibid.

14. Interview with Father Carlos Bravo, S.J., editor of *Christus*, Mexico City, November 6, 1990.

15. *Documentación e información católica (Dic)* 17, no. 23 (June 8, 1989).

16. In early 1991, the Holy See suspended CLAR's statutory right to select its own leaders. Henceforth, the organization will be headed by a Vatican appointee, who may veto any CLAR publication on moral, pastoral, or doctrinal matters; see *Latin American Weekly Report,* March 21, 1991, p. 9.

17. Other bishops associated with the progressive or liberationist current are Adalberto Almeida Merino (Chihuahua), Bartolomé Carrasco Briseño (Oaxaca), the late José A. Llaguno Farias (Tarahumara), José Pablo Rovalo Azcué (bishop emeritus of Zacatecas), and Serafín Velázquez Elizalde (Ciudad Gúzman); see, *Excélsior,* February 27, 1990, and interview with Bravo, November 6, 1990.

18. Oswaldo Sagastegui in *Excélsior,* February 1, 1979, p. 7–A.

19. Goulet, "The Mexican Church," 321.

20. Father Bravo suggests that Mexico's bishops developed submissive tendencies in the seminary, where they often studied under strong rectors; interview, November 6, 1990.

21. Prigione says that he has participated in the selection of between one-third and one-half of Mexico's bishops; interview, Mexico City, August 5, 1991. Father Bravo places the figure at 40 percent; interview, November 6, 1990. All told, there are 111 bishops: 93 active, 18 emeriti.

22. Interview with Archbishop Jerónimo Prigione, apostolic delegate, Mexico City, June 18, 1990.

23. Ibid., August 5, 1991.

24. Ibid., June 18, 1990.

25. *Excélsior,* November 30, 1988.

26. Prigione jokes that the *Priistas* are the "best" tennis players; interview, August 5, 1991.

27. Ibid.

28. Interview with Prigione, June 18, 1990.

29. René Delgado, "Delegado prigione: notas autobiográficas," *Este País,* no. 3 (June 1991): 22.

30. Interview with Prigione, August 5, 1991.

31. Businessman Jorge Martínez y Gómez del Campo had served as an unofficial liaison between several Mexican chief executives, including López Portillo, and the Vatican.

32. Camp, "Religious Elites in Mexico," 7.

33. Ibid., 12–16.

34. Ibid., 10.

35. Interview with Mons. Francisco Antonio Macedo Tenllado, chancellor, Pastoral Curia of the Archdiocese of Mexico City, Mexico City, June 12, 1990.

36. *Daily Press* (Newport News, Va.), September 21, 1985, p. C–5.

37. Comment to a foreign diplomat who asked to remain anonymous.

38. *New York Times,* March 31, 1935, p. 20.

39. Frank Brandenburg, "Los partidos políticos en méxico," cited in Otto Granados Roldán, *La iglesia católica mexicana como grupo de presión* (Mexico City: UNAM, 1981), 41.

40. Granados Roldán, *La iglesia católica mexicana,* 42.

41. *Excélsior,* April 24, 1990, p. 43–A. The church representative supplied no percentage for middle-class students.

42. *Excélsior,* April 24, 1990, p. 43–A.

43. *New York Times,* October 25, 1989.

44. Loaeza-Lajous, "Continuity and Change in the Mexican Catholic Church," 291.

45. Soledad Loaeza, "Iglesia católica y reformismo autoritario," *Foro internacional* 25, no. 2 (October–December 1984): 150–151, n. 31.

46. For instance, Ing. Guillermo Bustamante Manilla of the National Parents' Union placed the organization's membership at approximately 2 million members and Arancelí Montes, secretary of the Pro-Life Committee, estimated that her group boasted 2.7 million affiliates in 140 local committees. These

figures were obtained in telephone interviews conducted, respectively, on June 14 and June 19, 1990.

47. Quoted in *El Financiero,* May 7, 1990, p. 61.

48. *Contenido,* June 1981, 39–45.

49. Alan Riding, *Distant Neighbors* (New York: Alfred Knopf, 1985), 109.

50. *Contenido,* June 1981, p. 37.

51. *Latin American Weekly Report,* March 21, 1991, p. 9.

Chapter 3

1. Dennis M. Hanratty, "The Political Role of the Mexican Catholic Church: Contemporary Issues," *Thought* 59 (June 1984): 168–169.

2. Bailey, "The Church since 1940," 238.

3. Daniel H. Levine, "Religion, the Poor and Politics in Latin America Today," in Levine, ed., *Religion and Political Conflict in Latin America* (Chapel Hill: University of North Carolina Press, 1986), 11.

4. Ibid.

5. Edward L. Cleary, *In Crisis and Change: The Church in Latin America Today* (Maryknoll, N.Y.: Orbis Books, 1985), 42.

6. James N. Goodsell, "Mexico: Why the Students Rioted," *Current History* 56 (January 1969): 32–33.

7. Interview with Genaro Alamilla Arteaga, president, Episcopal Commission on Social Communications, November 5, 1990, Mexico City; Alamilla, who was CEM's secretary general during the Echeverría administration, recalls numerous meetings between government and church authorities that were "somewhat hidden, secret, and mysterious." Typically held in private homes, these sessions involved such questions as education and the status of foreign priests.

8. Loaeza, "Iglesia católica y reformismo autoritario," 154. The Mexican bishops published a letter in response to *Humanae Vitae* that emphasized that families could exercise their right of conscience in deciding the number of children they wished.

9. G. Pope Atkins, *Latin America in the International Political System,* 2nd ed. (Boulder, Colo.: Westview Press, 1989), 346–347.

10. Loaeza, "Iglesia católica y reformismo autoritario," 155, including n. 44.

11. Interview with Alamilla, November 5, 1990.

12. Interview with Guillermo Schulenburg Prado, abbot of the Basilica of Guadalupe, Mexico City, August 7, 1991.

13. Loaeza, "Iglesia católica y reformismo autoritario," 156–157.

14. Partido Revolucionario Institucional, "Memorandum sobre las relaciones estado-iglesia católica," Mexico City, November 1988, p. 24.

15. John J. Bailey, *Governing Mexico: The Statecraft of Crisis Management* (New York: St. Martin's Press, 1988), 112–113.

16. J. Bryan Hehir, "Papal Foreign Policy," *Foreign Policy,* no. 78 (Spring 1990): 36.

17. Ibid., 44.

18. *Washington Post,* January 9, 1979, p. A–12.

19. *Proceso,* July 13, 1981, pp. 18–19.

20. Ignacio Méndez Torres, *Celam-puebla 79: ¿desilusión o esperanza?* (Mexico City: Diana, 1980), 162–163.

21. "A New Church: From Medellín to Puebla," in Cleary, *In Crisis and Change,* 47.

22. Ernesto Cardinal Corripio A. and auxiliary bishops, *¿Cristianos por un partido marxista?* (n.p., n.d.), 7.

23. *Proceso,* November 22, 1982, pp. 24–26.

24. *Excélsior,* June 17, 1983, pp. 1, 12.

25. Hanratty, "The Political Role of the Mexican Catholic Church," 180.

26. *Unomásuno,* March 7, 1983, p. 5, cited in Hanratty, "The Political Role of the Mexican Catholic Church," 180.

27. *Excélsior,* June 3, 1986, pp. 4–A, 23–A.

28. *Unomásuno,* July 13, 1986, pp. 1, 9, cited in Dennis M. Hanratty, "Church-State Relations in Mexico in the 1980s," October 1986 (mimeo.), 15–16.

29. Interview with Prigione, June 18, 1990.

30. Lawrence Littwin, "Mexico: From Revolution to Corporate State," in Littwin, ed., *Latin American Catholicism and Class Conflict* (Encino, Calif.: Dickenson Publishing Company, 1974), 58.

31. *Unomásuno,* January 4, 1986, p. 5, cited in Hanratty, "Church-State Relations in Mexico in the 1980s," 17–18.

32. *Excélsior,* January 24, 1985, pp. 4–A, 27–A, and February 16, 1985, p. 2A–2, cited in Hanratty, "Church-State Relations in Mexico in the 1980s," 18.

33. Hanratty, "Church-State Relations in Mexico in the 1980s," 20.

34. Camp, "Religious Elites in Mexico," 4.

35. Loaeza-Lajous, "Continuity and Change in the Mexican Catholic Church," 294.

Chapter 4

1. Reportedly, in a survey of 500 deputies, senators, governors, high-level state officials, and PRI leaders, only 94 favored Salinas as the party's nominee. Enjoying greater support were then-Energy Secretary Alfredo del Mazo (167) and Government Secretary Manuel Bartlett Díaz (148); see, *Proceso,* October 19, 1987, pp. 12–15.

2. According to a *Los Angeles Times* poll (August 20, 1989), less than 25 percent of the respondents thought that Salinas had actually captured the 1988 contest.

3. George W. Grayson, "Mexico: A New Political Reality," *Current History* 87 (December 1988): 410.

4. His brother, Agustín Legorreta, formerly headed the Mexican Businessmen's Council, the country's most important business organization.

5. *Los Angeles Times,* August 20, 1989.

6. For a concise description of the 1989 Electoral Reform Law, see Roderic Ai Camp, "Mexico, 1989," in James Malloy and Eduardo Gamarra, eds., *Latin American and Caribbean Contemporary Record* 8 (1990).

7. *Los Angeles Times,* August 20, 1989.

8. Ibid.

9. Luis Narro Rodríguez, "¿Que valoran los mexicanos hoy?" in Alberto Hernández Medina et al., *Como somos los mexicanos* (Mexico City: CREA, 1987), 34, cited in Roderic Ai Camp, "Political Modernization in Mexico, Through a Looking Glass," to be published in Jaime O. Rodríguez, ed., *Political Evolution in Mexico* (Los Angeles: UCLA Latin American Studies Center, forthcoming).

10. *Nexos,* April 1990, pp. 57–60.

11. Rodríguez, "¿Que valoran los mexicanos hoy?" 34.

12. Interview with Prigione, August 5, 1991.

13. PRI, "Memorandum sobre las relaciones estado-iglesia católica," 11. The author wrote of a monopoly on *"creencias,"* which I translated as beliefs.

14. Ibid., 12–13.

15. Ibid., 15.

16. Ibid., 5.

17. Ibid.

18. *Proceso*, February 19, 1990, p. 7. Lest it appear that Salinas succeeded in co-opting Alameida and his colleagues, it should be noted that, in early May, the seven Chihuahua bishops issued a statement, "Pastoral Orientations on the Elections," in which they stressed the undesirability of single party control of the political process because of the ultimate danger of totalitarianism; see *NC News Service,* May 8, 1988.

19. Also attending were the president and vice president of the Conference of Mexican Bishops, Bishops Suárez Rivera and Juan Jesús Posadas Ocampo; CEM Secretary General Manuel Perez Gil; and the abbot of the Basilica of Guadalupe, Guillermo Schulenburg Prado.

20. *Proceso,* February 19, 1990, p. 7.

21. *Excélsior,* December 3, 1988.

22. *NC News Service,* April 19, 1989.

23. *Proceso,* February 19, 1990, p. 8.

24. Ibid., January 29, 1990, p. 15.

25. Ibid.

26. Ibid., January 1, 1990, p. 15.

27. *Excélsior,* June 14, 1991, pp. 1–A, 28–A.

28. Interview with Schulenberg Prado, August 7, 1991.

29. *Washington Post,* January 9, 1979, p. A–12.

30. Interview with Macedo Tenllado, June 12, 1990; interview with Schulenberg Prado, August 7, 1991.

31. Interview with Macedo Tenllado, June 12, 1990.

32. José López Portillo, *Mis tiempos: biografía y testimonio político,* part 1 (Mexico City: Fernández Editores, 1988), 129.

33. Interview with Macedo Tenllado, June 12, 1990. Mons. Macedo expressed a belief that Masonry is especially strong in the armed forces and the ministries of Education and Interior.

He also told me that a Masonic leader had indicated, before Salinas's inauguration, that only one president in recent years had not been a Mason. Although no name was mentioned, Mons. Macedo believes that the exception was Gustavo Díaz Ordaz (1964–1970).

34. Interview with Prigione, June 18, 1990.

35. *El Financiero,* May 7, 1990, p. 1.

36. Interview with Otto Granados Roldán, director of Social Communications, Presidency of Mexico, Mexico City, June 13, 1990.

37. Interview with Alamilla, November 5, 1990.

38. *Facts on File,* May 18, 1990, p. 371.

39. Interview with Prigione, August 5, 1991.

40. The government reported that PRI candidate Ramón Aguirre, former Mexico City mayor, soundly defeated PAN nominee Vicente Fox, a squeaky-clean businessman in Guanajuato. Fox attributes his loss to PRI-inspired irregularities in 700 of the state's 3,853 polling places. In 200 precincts, he said, more people voted than were registered; in another 200, the PRI claimed to have captured every ballot cast. In the face of these charges, Governor-elect Aguirre declined to take office, clearing the way for a new election.

41. Interview with Macedo Tenllado, June 12, 1990.

42. Interview with Alamilla, November 5, 1990.

43. Interview with Prigione, June 18, 1990.

44. Interview with Bravo, November 6, 1990.

45. *Latin American Weekly Report* (Latin American Newsletters, Ltd., London), May 24, 1990, p. 4.

46. Foreign Broadcast Information Service (FBIS), *Daily Report (Latin America)*, May 9, 1990, p. 11.

47. Ibid., 12.

48. *El Financiero,* May 14, 1990, p. 60.

49. Ibid.

50. *El Universal,* June 13, 1991, pp. 1, 14. In recalling the rhetoric that PARM Deputy Jaime Hernández employed in defending him in Congress, the combative Prigione dismissed the PPS, which still "weeps because of Stalin's death," as "four cats meowing at the moon in search of publicity." The apostolic delegate made certain that the new, liberal Soviet law on

religion was distributed to key members of Congress so, inter alia, the PPS could observe the tolerance practiced in Russia; interview with Prigione, August 5, 1991.

51. *El Financiero,* May 14, 1990, p. 60.

52. Interview with Prigione, June 18, 1990.

53. *Documentación e información católica (Dic)* 19, no. 28 (July 11, 1991): 423–426.

54. FBIS, *Daily Report (Latin America),* May 8, 1990, p. 10.

55. *Relaciones estado-iglesia* (Church-state relations) appeared in *El Universal,* February 25, 1990.

56. *Proceso,* January 29, 1990, p. 14.

57. Ibid., 15.

58. *Latin American Weekly Report,* June 28, 1990, pp. 6–7.

59. Interview with Prigione, August 5, 1991.

60. *Latin American Weekly Report,* June 28, 1990, pp. 6–7.

61. Americas Watch, *Human Rights in Mexico: A Policy of Impunity* (New York: Americas Watch, 1990).

62. *Excélsior,* June 9, 1990, p. 36–A.

63. Quoted in FBIS, *Daily Report (Latin America)*, November 13, 1991, p. 27.

64. *New York Times,* December 20, 1991, p. A–1.

65. *Proceso,* February 24, 1992, p. 15.

66. Ibid., 10–11.

67. FBIS, *Daily Report (Latin America)* December 27, 1991, p. 7.

68. *Latin American Regional Reports (Mexico and Central America)* (Latin American Newsletters, Ltd., London), May 7, 1992, p. 2.

69. Ibid.

CSIS BOOKS of Related Interest

The Mexico Series

Strategic Sectors in Mexican-U.S. Free Trade
M. Delal Baer and Guy F. Erb, editors

This monograph analyzes the economic impact of a Mexican-U.S. free trade agreement (FTA) on two strategically vital industries—automotive (by James P. Womack) and electronics (by Susan Walsh Sanderson and Ricardo Zermeño—González.) Alan Stoga, in his chapter "Beyond Coexistence: The United States and Mexico," looks into the strategic rationale behind the U.S. decision to enter into an FTA with Mexico.

ISBN 0-89206-172-3 $9.95   1991

The Mexican Labor Machine
George W. Grayson
ISBN 0-89206-131-6 $7.95   1989

The Congress and Mexico: Bordering on Change
A Report of the CSIS Congressional Study Group on Mexico
Senators Lloyd Bentsen and Pete Wilson, Representatives Ronald Coleman and Jim Kolbe, cochairmen
ISBN 0-89206-144-8 $6.95   1989

Mexico and the United States: Leadership Transitions and the Unfinished Agenda
M. Delal Baer, editor
ISBN 0-89206-115-4 $6.95   1988

CSIS Bookroom 1800 K Street, N.W. Suite 400 Washington, D.C. 20006